EMBRACE THE POWER OF YOU

EMBRACE THE

POWER OF YOU

Owning Your Identity at Work

TRICIA MONTALVO TIMM

Praise for *Embrace the Power of You*

Mentor vs. Sponsors comparison used with permission from SLAC National Accelerator Laboratory.

Cataloguing in publication information is available from Library and Archives Canada.
ISBN 978-1-77458-257-2 (paperback/hardcover)
ISBN 978-1-77458-258-9 (ebook)

Page Two
pagetwo.com

Edited by Emily Schultz
Cover and interior design by Jennifer Lum
Printed and bound TKTK
Distributed by TKTK

21 22 23 24 25 5 4 3 2 1

www.triciatimm.com

To all those who have
ever felt like an "other."

Contents

Introduction

"MY MOM is from El Salvador. My dad is from Ecuador. I am Latina."

That is how I started my LinkedIn post. It was the first time I had ever posted anything publicly about my heritage. The other posts had been about the recent acquisition I had managed, a board I had been appointed to or topics I was passionate about, but never anything personal. Never anything about me being Latina. I kept that part of my identity under wraps through my entire career as a high-tech corporate attorney in Silicon Valley.

I spent hours carefully writing that short post, trying to find the right words. I thought that all of the people I had worked with all these years might be surprised to learn that I am Latina. My mind kept racing with fears about what they might think of me when they read my post.

"She is such a fraud."

"She is simply trying to leverage the diversity movement for her own personal benefit."

"Isn't it timely that she is calling herself Latina now when everyone is looking for diverse candidates."

I had built up such an expansive and impressive network of CEOs, board members and venture investors, and I was worried they would look down on me if I revealed this part of my identity. Executives were growing frustrated with the diversity conversation and I was afraid to alienate anyone. I was part of "the club" and didn't want to get kicked out. On the flipside, I had fears that the Latino community I was now hoping to serve would reject me for not having been an advocate for them before now. I felt shame and guilt and I was terrified of their potential response. Frankly, I am still working on forgiving myself for staying in the shadows for so long. But even with those fears looming inside me, I knew that talking about my identity and being unafraid to show up authentically would really help a lot of people. So, I forged ahead.

After re-reading my post several times, I decided that something was missing. I'm not sure why I thought people wouldn't believe that I was Latina, but I did. I felt like a fraud. I decided that I needed to include a picture of me with my aunts, uncles and cousins back in Ecuador. For reasons only my mind could make sense of, I was compelled to provide proof—photographic proof—that I was, in fact, Latina.

I clicked on the "Start a Post" prompt on LinkedIn. The famous words popped up: "What do you want to talk about?"

I wrote the words.

Added the photo.

Then paused.

I stared at that blue "Post" rectangle for what felt like hours. Was I brave enough? Was I willing to jeopardize my status? Would I be okay if I was rejected?

I decided that, yes, I would be okay. So, with a large, deep breath, I pushed the button.

Then I sat there, scared of the potential fallout from what I had just done.

What happened next completely shocked me. It was like out of the movies, when a social post goes viral across the screen in bubbles, but in my case it was in a good way. I started to get thumbs-up, hearts, claps, love—all the emojis. These were followed by connection requests from other Latinas who were thrilled to see someone like them on a professional networking platform. I got comments like:

"Thank you for sharing your story, Tricia! My mother is from El Salvador too."

"Love this! I'm also Ecuadorian. Glad we are connected."

"What a beautiful family. Thank you for sharing your story. My kids are watching."

The overwhelming support that ensued convinced me I had done the right thing. I knew that, while it may have taken me a long time and a lot of healing to get to this place, it was my time to serve this community. Very few Latinas had made it to the top ranks of corporate America, so I felt like I had a responsibility to be visible.

Millions of people from all walks of life are hiding a piece of their identity in order to fit in to mainstream society. They were either taught by their parents to assimilate quickly or shown by the media what "normal" means, and it looks like nothing like them. Because of these influences, those who consider themselves different have been socialized that, in order to make it, the best thing to do is to conform to the culture around them to fit in and make everyone else comfortable. Eventually, this process of changing who you are becomes too much, and many fall prey to anxiety, depression and burnout. They exit the workforce or refuse to bring their whole selves to work out of self-preservation. The real loss is to all of us. What opportunities are we missing out on if someone decides to stay hidden?

The cure for cancer or the next technology breakthrough could be sitting right in front of us, but that person is too afraid to speak up. This is a tragedy.

Helping Latinas and anyone else who has ever felt marginalized or invisible is now my life's purpose. I have had the unique privilege of sitting on both sides of the table. I have been a C-suite executive and sat in boardrooms, so I have the opportunity to engage in difficult yet meaningful conversations in a way that people who are used to thinking in business terms can understand and accept. I have also experienced what it feels like to be overlooked, excluded and made to feel invisible, so I know how real the struggle is for so many.

Despite a perception that Latinas are making progress in corporate America, the statistics show otherwise. After twenty-five years in high tech, I know that I am one of the very few Latinas who has made it to the general counsel seat, become a board director and cracked the venture capital ceiling. The share of general counsels who are Latinas is around 2 percent, the share of Latinas who are corporate directors is around 1 percent and the share of Latinas who are in venture capital is around 0.2 percent.

To gain the courage to make that LinkedIn post was not easy. As a first-generation professional in the high-tech world, I quickly learned that I was not like the others. I always felt like I didn't belong, and I desperately tried to change the parts of me that were different to try to fit in. It only made things worse. I quickly became exhausted from constantly trying to be someone I was not. I grew frustrated, tired and bitter. After two decades of hiding and conforming, I finally realized that, in order to belong, I first needed to accept who I was. I realized that belonging begins with self-acceptance—and that once I was able to embrace all the parts of me, love myself and recognize what value I bring, others would begin to see it too.

Since that LinkedIn post, I have been invited to speak and share my story at companies, women's groups, Latina organizations and many events. During each presentation, I talk about my parents, what it felt like to be the "only" or the "other" in the room and how much I had to hustle to climb the corporate ladder without a road map.

Every time, I see heads nodding in the audience.

Tears slowly falling down faces.

People often tell me it is the first time they have ever felt seen.

This is what prompted me to begin writing this book. Here, I will take you through my own personal journey toward self-acceptance. I will also share with you the stories of other top executive leaders who once hid parts of their identity in order to belong but ultimately made the difficult decision to stop hiding and show up authentically. I will hold your hand as you go through this journey, as it is not an easy one. Scattered throughout this book you will also find places to pause for self-reflection, or suggestions for action items that can help you take some small steps on your own path. These are important stops. At times, you may think to yourself, "I am not strong enough to do this." But stick with it, because by the end of this book you will have the tools to embrace what makes you unique and the courage to enter the world authentically.

By telling my story, I hope to inspire you to tell your own story. One story can make a difference.

How to Use This Book

A Note on Language

While I identify as Latina, I want to acknowledge that not all people like me use this term to refer to themselves. Some use the term Hispanic. Others use Latinx or Latine in order to be gender neutral. Yet others combine terms, such as "Hispanic/ Latino," which you often see in studies and surveys. The truth is that, as a community, we span a broad range of race, identities, skin color, languages, history and customs. In this book, I refer to myself as Latina and the community as Latino because the Spanish language assigns the male gender to plurals (yes— another touchy topic for another book!). In using Latino as a group term, please know that my intent is to include everyone.

Self-Reflection Moments

Throughout this book, you will find a series of "Self-Reflections." These are designed for you to take the information you just read, and explore how you connect with it. They will give you the opportunity to pause for a moment before you move on, so you can do some deeper reflection about your own life. As you go through some of the questions in these Self-Reflection Moments, you may uncover things about yourself and your life that you hadn't realized before, and these new pieces of understanding may come as a surprise to you. In some moments, you may not fully understand what you are feeling. It has taken me years to unpack so much of my story and, in fact, I am still unpacking. As you go through this book and your own journey, you may also uncover things that you will want to remember and unpack later, so you may find it handy to keep a journal nearby and write down your thoughts or learnings as you go.

Next Small Thing

You will also periodically find "Next Small Thing" suggestions. These suggestions were inspired by Glennon Doyle, who asks her listeners to do "the next right thing" in her podcast *We Can Do Hard Things*. The action items you will find throughout this book are designed to help you take the ideas you just read and use them to implement change in your own life. The goal of each "Next Small Thing" is that these actions are exactly that—small. They should feel doable and not something you are worried you might fail at. Still, in some cases, they may feel too big. That is okay too. There is no right or wrong. These actions are simply suggestions of ways you could start making a small change today.

Manager Strategies

This book is for those who struggle to belong. However, if you are a leader or a manager who is trying to learn more about belonging and how to create an inclusive workplace, this book will help you too. You will see first-hand what it is like to feel invisible. To feel unseen. To want to fit in. My hope for you is that, by reading this book, you will foster a newfound empathy for those in your organization who desperately want to contribute but are afraid to bring their full selves to work. For you, I have closed each chapter with specific and actionable items that you as a manager can take to create a more inclusive environment. I have also created workshops and other programs you can bring into your organization to help you continue this work—you can find out more about these resources in the back of this book.

1

Who Is the Real You?

MY HEART is racing so fast that I'm sure everyone around me can see it beating out of my body.

I practice my relaxation techniques. Close my eyes. Slowly take three deep breaths.

I enter the stairwell on my way to the conference room where I am about to deliver my story to the whole company. The talk had actually been my own idea but, in this moment, I regret suggesting it.

Alone in the stairwell, I stop and pause. Another deep breath.

I remember a quote from the poet Maya Angelou: "I come as one, but I stand as ten thousand."

You may feel alone, I remind myself, *but you stand as ten thousand.*

I arrive in the conference room and watch our employees gather. I smile. You know that fake smile, like everything is totally okay and that you've got this? I'm the general counsel of a hot Silicon Valley tech company for God's sake. Why wouldn't I have this?

The clock inches toward the top of the hour. Time for me to start. The CEO takes a seat in the front row. I glance at him. He gives me a slight nod and a smile and I breathe a little bit easier. I begin.

———————————

The road to that moment was not easy. It was National Hispanic Day at Looker, a data analytics software company in Santa Cruz, California. This is where I told my story for the first time.

My parents are both immigrants to this country. They met in Los Angeles and worked several jobs to make a life for themselves. For them, success was defined by providing their children with a better life and a good education.

When I was born, we lived in a predominantly Latino community in Los Angeles. My parents managed an apartment building, which allowed them to live rent-free and gave them a chance to save up for a house. When my sister and I were about to start elementary school, they wanted us to have the opportunity to get a better education, so they moved us out of the city and into the suburbs, and enrolled us in a local Catholic school.

My mom used to say to me, "They can always take away your things, but they can never take away your education." I am not sure who "they" were in this advice, but it was something that was drilled into my head every day. Education would be my ticket to the American dream.

My school was predominantly white with very few Latinos and even fewer Black students. All of our teachers and coaches were white, and I quickly realized that my family was different. My parents had thick Spanish accents. We had relatives in faraway countries and our traditions and celebrations were different from those of my classmates. Even at that young age, I picked up on these differences.

As I started every new chapter of my life, I kept conformity as my guiding principle. I was usually the only person of color in the room and many times the only woman. The skills I learned in grade school to keep from standing out, such as adapting my clothes and hairstyle to the accepted fashion or laughing or staying silent at uncomfortable remarks, served me well in my professional world.

I had the routine down cold: walk into a room, scan it and then adapt. I call this the "Scan-Evaluate-Adapt" process.

How many women are in the room?

Are there any people of color here?

Am I the youngest or oldest person?

These were all very important questions as I figured out how to show up in gatherings or approach conversations. Most of the time I instinctively knew that I could not show up as the loud Latina girl who liked to share her opinion confidently.

I quickly figured out which persona needed to be present in any given situation. What sport do I need to be able to talk about? What hobbies should I be interested in? Do I like red or white wine? If red, is it a cab or pinot? In order for me to fit into the traditional corporate setting, I needed to have shared likes and experiences with those around me. Talking about tamales, sangria and mariachis would simply not cut it. Not if I wanted to advance.

I learned to assimilate to my environment as a result of my experience of being the "only." Either the "only" woman, the "only" Latino or the "only" working mom. If you have ever felt like the "only" of something or like an "other" in the room, you know how lonely it feels. So, instead of standing out and having the spotlight on your "otherness," you have likely gone through the experience of downplaying or hiding that piece of your identity that you believe may not be welcomed in a given situation.

The most common identities we think about are race, gender, ethnicity and sexual orientation. But anybody can be an "other." It can be the single mom who struggles to keep it all together at home but pretends to be totally fine. It can be the executive with a learning disability who doesn't want others to know that reading or spelling is hard for him. Or it can be a manager who battles anxiety and depression but doesn't want to ask for time off for fear that her team may think she can't handle the workload. Many of us worry that, if we showed our true self, we would not be accepted. All of these fears are real and often push us toward hiding those parts of our identity.

I Feel Like an Outsider

Mastering the skill of hiding took time, but I got a crash course during my first job out of law school. I started my career at one of the largest and most elite corporate law firms in the country. This was a traditional firm that had large corner offices, mahogany desks, tall tinted windows and boardrooms with whiteboards and conference phones. The firm represented some of the oldest companies in the country, such as institutional banks that backed hot Silicon Valley start-ups. I was incredibly fortunate to have launched my career at a law firm with this distinct reputation and a long list of brand-name clients.

As I started my first week in the fall of 1996, the firm distributed an announcement that listed all of the new first-year associates. It included our names, a photo and the law school that each of us attended. As I scrolled through each page, I read the school names out loud: Stanford, Harvard, UCLA, Cornell. *How did I end up among this elite group of associates?* I wondered. As I continued to scroll, I also noticed that I was the only Latina. While I knew on an intellectual level that a firm like this one would not hire me out of pity, it sure felt like I somehow landed the position by accident. I think that this is where my imposter syndrome started. But I kept my head down, embraced the opportunity and decided to work hard to prove that I belonged among this group of incredibly talented first-year associates.

The law firm was made up of mostly white older men. Everybody was welcoming and, in fact, my first manager was a wonderful man who taught me how to be an exceptional lawyer. But his life was nothing like mine, so it was hard to form a meaningful relationship with him other than that of manager/employee. This was the case with most of the partners I worked with.

And while I certainly did face moments of bias and exclusion, that is not what was really hard. It was more the absence of anyone like me that quietly made me feel like an outsider. Only a handful of women were senior leaders or partners at the firm, and we never heard about their families or their struggles to balance it all. I only remember one Latino who was a senior associate, and I always wondered if we had similar life stories.

My existence as a young Latina lawyer was very lonely. I had to forge ahead on my own. I had to figure out the rules of the game without any guidance.

While I soon mastered the skill of fitting in and looking like I belonged in the room, I never *felt* like I belonged. When you don't see anyone in the room who looks like you then you don't feel like you belong. Everybody else seems to be able to share the same jokes, the same childhood memories, the same opinions, the same taste in food, but yours is different. So, you stay quiet, smile and go along with it. It seemed relatively simple and really the only way to navigate this new world.

Everyone Seems Like They Belong Here, Except Me

As I progressed through that first year at the law firm, I looked for things that felt or sounded familiar, but there was not much I could relate to. I was not an avid golfer. I did not have a love for sushi or shrimp. I did not enjoy wearing suits. In fact, the only time I felt truly comfortable in that building was at night, when I could put my hair up in a ponytail, kick off my heels and enjoy my nightly chat with the janitor.

As a first-year associate at a large corporate law firm, you pretty much work all the time. Back in the 1990s, we did not bring computers home so we would just stay at the firm late into the evening. For me, that was usually around 11 p.m. A funny thing happens at night at a law firm. As the clock gets to 6 p.m., the staff and partners begin to shuffle home to their families. The phones and fax machines stop ringing and the hustle and bustle of the day starts to slowly dissipate. And, suddenly, it becomes quiet. Generally, the only people left in the office are the first- and second-year associates trying to make sense of the crazy day that just finished. Every evening during my first year, we would all slowly emerge from our offices like toddlers peeking their heads out of their bedrooms after lights out—often, simply looking for someone to commiserate with.

Little by little, people trickled home, but I did not. I was usually the one that stayed at the office the latest. I was determined to make it as a lawyer no matter how hard it was. I learned this work ethic from my parents. Every evening I would enjoy a small moment around 9 p.m., when the janitorial crew would come by. Often, it was one particular older Latino gentleman who would come into my office to clean out my garbage can. I remember smiling and saying hello to him in Spanish every night.

"¡Hola! ¿Cómo estás esta noche?"

I remember the first time I said hello to him. He looked surprised that I spoke to him, especially in Spanish. I'm not sure many, if any, of the associates, every really talked to him, but I did. We would chat for a moment; he would empty my wastebasket and then go on to the next office. There was something familiar about his voice and his mannerisms that made my body relax and feel at ease.

I would often think about his family, since his shift started so late in the evening. I wondered whether he had children and whether he had to leave them behind to go to work at night. My dad also worked evenings when I was growing up, so he reminded me so much of him. I admired this man for his work ethic and for doing a job that most did not want. I liked acknowledging him and thanking him every night for keeping our offices clean.

Looking back, I felt more comfortable talking with the cleaning crew than I did talking with the law firm partners. Eventually, I came to believe that I was not worthy enough to be an associate at this prestigious firm. When you don't see or relate to anyone else in the room and you believe that you do not deserve to be there, you soon assume that everyone else belongs there except you.

SELF-REFLECTION MOMENT

- Take a look at your workplace environment. Who do you see in leadership positions?

- Who do you feel most comfortable interacting with at work? Is it a colleague who has a similar lived experience as you? Is it with the support or service staff? Or is it a member of the leadership team? Notice when you are most comfortable being your true self.

- If there is no setting at work where you feel comfortable, that is okay as well. At this point, it is just data about you and your work environment.

Hiding My Identity Makes Me Feel Lonely

It wasn't too hard for me to hide my ethnic identity. As a lighter-skinned Latina, I could often pass as white. It was even easier after I got married and went from "Patricia Montalvo" to "Tricia Timm."

I held the belief that if I hid or downplayed my ethnicity I would progress in the workplace. I was surprised to learn that I was not alone in feeling this way. According to the Center for Talent Innovation, 76 percent of Latinos expend energy on repressing parts of their personas in the workplace. They cover or downplay who they are, and modify their appearance, their body language, their communication style and their leadership presence.

Another unfortunate consequence of hiding is that others around you are uninhibited about what they say. I sat in silence more times that I care to admit as people around me made jokes about my ethnic background without knowing they were talking about me. A little bit of my identity was lost every time a classmate would say a derogatory remark about Latinos, a co-worker expressed frustration about diversity efforts in the workplace or a soccer mom complained about the injustice of affirmative action in the college application process. All of these societal and cultural moments kept reinforcing the message to me that I was somehow "lesser than" those around me.

Despite all the success I had earned with my hard work and perseverance, I did not feel entitled to it. As a member of an underrepresented group, I internalized the belief that I somehow got an unfair advantage because of affirmative action programs or diversity mandates. And as this belief worked its way inside me, I came to question whether I deserved all my success, despite my hard work. I started to wonder if I had genuinely earned everything I had achieved, and if I belonged in the room after all. This led to self-doubt and my need to prove myself at all costs.

The weight of hiding who you are is heavy. You can lug it around for a long time, but after a while the loneliness and shame start to overshadow your everyday life. It took me two decades to realize this.

I went through each stage of life like a checklist. *Head down, keep up the pretense and don't rock the boat.* I kept going and never looked up.

- ☑ Graduate high school
- ☑ Graduate college
- ☑ Graduate law school
- ☑ Join big law firm
- ☑ Get married
- ☑ Have kids
- ☑ Become general counsel

On paper, this looked like success. But these checkmarks do not show all the bumps, bruises and tears it took to get there.

I want to pause here and acknowledge the tremendous privilege I've had in my life. I had two parents who decided to stay married and raise their kids together. They intentionally moved us into a middle-class neighborhood so that I could have a sense of safety. They worked multiple jobs to give me a first-class education, which ultimately led me to college and law school. I am keenly aware that not everyone gets these opportunities. Some of you may have grown up in the foster care system. Some of you may have been raised in a low-income community and as a result experienced higher levels of violence, lacked access to affordable health care or attended under-resourced schools. Some of you may have grown up in wealthy homes and what appeared to be the perfect family but, behind closed doors, family members battled with mental health conditions or addiction. Some of you may have been a child of divorced parents. I recognize that the playing field is not level and some of us started ahead of others. But, as I will explain later in this book, no matter what obstacle or boulder was put in front of you, overcoming that challenge and wanting a better life for yourself has created a resilience in you that you don't even know you have. Stick with me on this journey, because I know that you too can get to a place where you will lovingly embrace who you are and where you came from, and realize that your unique perspective adds tremendous value and is exactly what is needed in the world right now.

Beginning with Self-Acceptance

After twenty years I had completed all of the items on my life checklist. I had overcome all odds to get there. The number of Latinas who attend a four-year university is small to begin with. If you take that group and track how many go to law school, that number gets even smaller. Few pass the bar and hardly any join a corporate law firm. If you, like me, beat all odds and join a corporate law firm or in-house legal department, once you get there, there is no one that looks like you or few that sponsor you. But for me, instead of feeling proud of all my achievements, I was lost. I had spent my whole life seeking everyone else's acceptance but my own. During school I had changed my appearance and style to appear like the other students. As an attorney, I adapted my social likes and dislikes to integrate with the corporate culture around me. As a working parent, I pretended not to be devoted to my children while at work, and on the soccer field I pretended not to be an accomplished lawyer. All the time, I feared being judged by everyone around me, and I spent all my energy trying to maintain each different facade. I was emotionally and physically exhausted, but I didn't understand why.

As I was starting to work on improving my own sense of self, I discovered the work of Brené Brown and read this quote in her book *The Gifts of Imperfection*: "Because true belonging only happens when we present our authentic, imperfect selves to the world, our sense of belonging can never be greater than our level of self-acceptance."

It was like one of Oprah Winfrey's "ah-ha moments." As soon as I read that definition, I realized that I was thinking about belonging in the wrong way. I recognized that, in order for me to belong in any room, I must first begin with accepting and loving who I am. For my entire life, I had kept wanting approval from others to validate my worth. I would say things like:

"If they just listened to me."

"If they just invited me to that event."

"If they just included me in that conversation or asked for my opinion."

Then *they* would see who I really was and the value I bring. I wanted people around me to invite me into the room. The journey to believing that my authentic self was good enough was a long one. In fact, I would say that it never ends for some of us. Whenever I try something new, all of the doubts and fears come rushing back and I have to remind myself of all the lessons and tools that I will describe throughout this book. I need this book as much as you do.

The exact moment I decided to make change in my life came on a random day, out of nowhere. I knew that keeping up the disguise of a fully put-together mom, lawyer, spouse, sibling, parent and daughter was too much, but it all came to a crashing halt one evening on a drive home.

I don't even recall where I was coming from, but I remember that my husband had committed us to another dinner party at our house that evening and I had to get home to be the dutiful wife and host. I turned the corner to enter our neighborhood and caught sight of my friend Gina's house. At the time, she had just begun work as a conscious leadership coach. She had taught me some techniques that gave me permission to express emotions, including the ugly ones such as anger and sadness that I would normally keep suppressed.

In an instant, instead of turning the corner and heading to my house and the dinner party that awaited me, I slammed on the brakes and swung into her driveway. I walked up to her front door and knocked, not knowing if she was home.

"Hi, Tricia," she said. "What's up?"

"Are you home alone?" I asked her.

She responded that she was.

"Can I come in please? Dinner guests are arriving at my house right now and I just can't do it. I can't keep all this up anymore."

Nothing about this dinner party was particularly overwhelming. In fact, it was a casual BBQ and my husband was taking care of most of it. But it was the culmination of decades of doing what I was supposed to do rather than what I wanted to do that caught up to me in that moment. I felt like I was a volcano and that magma had been building up over a lifetime and the pressure was too strong now to keep it all inside. The lava was coming up and it was time for the volcano to explode.

At first, I explained to her my frustrations in a very matter-of-fact tone. Upset, but put together. She stopped me in the middle of it.

"You are not expressing your emotions. You are just telling me about them. Let it out."

"What do you mean?"

"You can actually use emotions like anger in a positive way. Moving it helps you overcome stress and challenges. It's called emotional intelligence. Just let out your anger."

I didn't know how to do that so I was hesitant at first. I was still trying to keep it all together. I started putting a little more of my emotion into the story, but Gina was not satisfied.

"Tricia, let it out."

"Are you sure?"

"Yes, just let it out. Scream, hit pillows, whatever you need to do. Just let it out."

And then it all came out. I told her about the shame I felt for hiding my ethnicity and for my failure to stand up to the bias and discrimination that surrounded me. I told her about how hard it was to simultaneously be the adoring, loving mom and the strong, dedicated businesswoman. I told her how I was drained from pretending to be the perfect wife, daughter and sister who could fix anything but needed nothing to be fixed herself. I kept talking and talking and she did not interrupt me. She sat there quietly and lovingly, letting the volcano explode until every last bit of lava had poured out. At the end, I burst into tears and she held me. In that moment I realized that if I didn't accept and love myself first—my real, raw, messy self— then how could I expect others to accept me?

Belonging begins with self-acceptance. It sounds simple, so why can't we just snap our fingers and say, "You're enough. You belong. Now, let's move on"? I wish it were that effortless. I wish that, now that you have this pearl of wisdom, you could immediately gain the sense of belonging that you are so yearning for. I imagine it could be that straightforward if you didn't spend decades hearing from the outside world that you aren't enough. Or if you hadn't spent most of your life hiding your true identity to fit in. The road to self-acceptance is not easy, but it is doable. It doesn't happen overnight. In fact, for me, it took a long time—but I started small. I started by making one small change, and then repeating it. I also started by changing things that wouldn't cost me too much, such as what I chose to wear to work—for example, instead of fancy black slacks, cream blouse and heels, I wore jeans, a sweater and my half boots. I wore my hair in my natural air-dried curly state instead of the clean-cut blowout and straightened hair I had become accustomed to for work. Over time, I gradually moved to higher-stakes items, such as combating racism at work and in my community. But, at the beginning, it was just the little things. Then, I repeated them.

Once you begin the process of accepting your true self, a whole new world starts to open up. I started saying "yes" to things I truly enjoyed, and, more importantly, saying "no" to things I did not enjoy. My friendships became more authentic, my marriage became more honest, and my work became more meaningful.

This personal journey has taught me that you do not need to spend endless amounts of energy hiding your true self from others. Instead, you can spend that energy on things that bring you joy, and you can surround yourself with people who accept you just as you are. When you are able to do this, ideas start to flow easier, relationships become deeper and opportunities start to come your way.

Embracing Your Authentic Self Will Lead You to What You Most Want

It wasn't until I truly accepted myself and started showing up authentically that things finally changed for me. I was in my mid-forties and had decided that I no longer wanted to do the general counsel thing anymore. I had worked at a top law firm, I had been the general counsel at a public company, and had helped build companies. I was frankly tired and needed some time to myself. I had decided to revive the legal consulting business I had started years earlier so that I could remain engaged in my profession but have more flexibility. It was during this

time that I unknowingly embarked on my own personal transformation, one that led to my awakening. I was living a simpler
life with no desire to go back into the corporate world when an
amazing job opportunity presented itself. You know the saying
"Luck is when opportunity meets preparation"? I believe this to
be true. I could say I was lucky to have joined Looker, but it was
really that I had been preparing for that moment my whole life.

It was 2017 and Looker was seeking its first general counsel.
I remember the interview process. By that point, I had determined that I was no longer going to pretend to be someone
different. I was committed to showing up as myself. If I didn't
get the job, it meant that it wasn't the right place for me. I would
not be disappointed by the rejection.

During the interview, instead of worrying about whether
they thought I was qualified enough to do the job, I spoke confidently about what I knew and how I could help them scale
the company. I talked about my kids and what they were up to
at school and the struggles of parenting. I was not concerned
if my laugh was too loud. I even had a great conversation with
the VP of HR about culture and belonging.

For so long, the concept of the general counsel of a Silicon
Valley high-tech company looked like a gray-haired older white
man in a tailored suit. I was the exact opposite of that and for
many years had to combat that bias—one held not only by others, but by me as well. But, at this Santa Cruz data analytics
company, myself as I am was exactly what they were looking
for! Had I conformed my behavior, mannerisms or opinions to
what I thought they wanted, I likely would not have landed that
job. Looker was perfectly okay with a confident, slightly loud
Latina with kids.

I knew that I had landed in the right job the first day I walked
into the Looker offices. I started the day before the winter break,
so things were a little chaotic. I began during an off-cycle, which

meant that my new-hire orientation was a little different from most. The first thing I saw as I entered the building was "The Kitchen Table," a large table where employees would gather to work or hang out. Music was playing in the background and, as I learned was typical, a couple of dogs were walking around. I immediately felt at ease in this casual environment.

Schools had already let out for winter break, so there were kids roaming around. A few school-aged kids were playing on their phones or reading a book, and some younger ones were scooting happily around the office. I looked around the open office space to see if anyone was annoyed by this, but no, everyone was just working like it was normal. Many had their headsets on and were typing away at their computers. Others were walking in the hallways or talking to colleagues, perhaps avoiding the kids but not bothered by them. I was amazed.

I thought back to those earlier days in my career when I kept my daughter's existence quiet, even secretly nursing her in the parking garage between company meetings. I reveled in the stark contrast of these two work environments, overjoyed that a workplace could look so different. Parents working here were allowed to be just that—working parents. They had permission to openly juggle their job and their kids, and to talk about how it was hard and required flexibility. There was no shame in caring about your family.

In those first few hours I learned everything I needed to learn about belonging. When employees can show up as their authentic selves, they come to work with excitement and purpose. When they feel seen and heard, they don't have to waste time or energy in changing their appearance, mannerisms or language, or fabricate an excuse for leaving early if they need to go watch their kid's events. All that energy wasted on hiding can instead be harnessed into producing high-quality work, and the extra time can be devoted to participating in life. While no company is perfect, this one had put value in belonging and was striving to create a place where people felt seen and heard.

The culture at Looker did not happen by accident. The founder was very intentional about creating a company where everyone felt welcome. One of their earliest values was, in the early days, called the "Island of Misfit Toys," named in honor of the animated Christmas adventure *Rudolph the Red-Nosed Reindeer*. The idea was that while some of us may be different (like Rudolph and his red nose), it is exactly our difference that makes us special. On this island—the Looker Island—we were all welcome, no matter how different we were. I remember hearing this value for the first time and smiling. I had fond memories of that film and identified with those misfit toys. We eventually changed the name of this corporate value to "Belonging" to better capture the inclusive essence of the environment Looker wanted to create. Although we had used the term affectionately, we came to realize that none of us are misfits.

Since Looker had fostered an inclusive space for its employees, I felt more comfortable showing up authentically. It was during my first weeks that I decided to tell the CEO a little bit about my background and the challenges I had faced as a young working mom. It was the first time I had ever shared personal parts of my life with a manager, let alone a CEO. Over the coming weeks, I would reveal more, and he would listen. Given my past corporate experiences, I was worried that he would either ignore my story and go on with the business at hand, or start walking on eggshells for fear of offending me. Instead, he told me how eye-opening my story was and, later, he asked me if I wanted to lead the company's first-ever diversity, equity and inclusion (DEI) program.

My courage to speak my truth in that moment led to the development of a DEI program that ultimately changed lives.

Looker had very little attrition and I believe that a large part of that was due to the inclusive nature of its workplace. Investing in its people and culture ultimately contributed to the company's success, and to its $2.6-billion sale to Google three years later.

Showing Up as Your Authentic Self Adds Value to Your Organization

Telling my story during National Hispanic Heritage month was a life-changing moment for me. The event took place only a few short months after I had told the CEO about my background. I had downplayed my heritage my entire career, so this was uncharted territory for me. The thought of not only revealing my ethnicity but shouting it from the rooftops was terrifying. Would the executive team treat me the same? Would my legal advice hold the same value? Would I get excluded from meetings? All sorts of "what-ifs" were circling my mind. But I did it anyway.

I had prepared a slide deck to tell my story because, hey, I'm lawyer so that's what I do. I began the presentation with some background information about my parents and where they came from, including a picture of each of their flags: El Salvador and Ecuador. I shared pictures of my very large and vibrant family in Ecuador at a family BBQ. I included two different headshots that I used in my brief days as an actress and recounted how I was forced to change my last name to be more "American." I represented the dichotomy I experienced while working in the law firm by showing pictures of white men golfing and a Latino janitor and asking which picture looked more like me. I confessed that I struggled to feel like I belonged anywhere.

At some point, I paused and looked around the room. Complete silence. Nobody was checking their phones and all eyes were fixed on me. Everybody was paying attention. As I scanned the room, I even noticed that several people were wiping away tears.

After the presentation, a line formed of people I knew and others I had never met. Many gave me hugs of support, but I distinctly remember one employee in particular. She was a young Latina, probably in her mid-twenties, who was working in customer support. She came up to me and broke down in tears.

"I just wanted to say, thank you," she told me. "Your story reminded me of my parents and abuelitos in Mexico. I know exactly how you felt because that is how I have felt before."

I stood there, amazed. Suddenly all my fears of revealing myself disappeared, and joy filled my body. I realized that by being vulnerable and sharing my story, I had helped her.

It was worth it.

"Seeing that you come from such a similar background as me and that you've made it to the top makes me feel like I can do that too and that I don't have to change anything about myself to get there," she told me with a smile. I saw so much gratitude in her eyes.

I did not realize what a profound impact telling my story would have on any one person. In that moment, I flashed back to the days when I saw no one who looked like me, and how lonely that felt. I thought about all the times that I had hidden details about my background as a Latina and a working parent and what a disservice that was for others. I was now someone that the next generation could look to for hope. By telling my story, I had made it so that she was no longer alone.

On that day, showing up as my authentic self at work gave permission for other Latino employees at my company to show up as their authentic selves too.

A company that ensures that all people are represented in its leadership makes varied identities normal and acceptable, reducing the need for any person working there to downplay their particular identity. Ultimately, if employees are able to bring their authentic selves to work, organizations will also thrive. When employees have a sense of belonging, they are engaged and productive. Organizations retain top talent and employee morale increases. A diverse workforce will be able to meet the demands of a global community by designing products and branding that appeal to customers that are reflective of our diverse world.

My hope is that, through this book, you will not only learn to embrace what makes you different, you will also feel seen and realize that your unique lived experience adds tremendous value. That you, showing up in the world exactly as yourself, are what the world needs right now.

MANAGER STRATEGIES

Many employees are struggling to fit in. They may not feel comfortable bringing their authentic self to work and, as a result, they are not creating a real connection with you or the company. Here are some tips on how to be a more inclusive leader.

Take a look at who is on your leadership team. There is a saying that goes: "You can't be what you can't see." If your leadership team is lacking representation at the top, then it is hard for those from underrepresented groups to feel like they can rise. Be intentional about increasing diversity at the highest level of the organization. One CEO I spoke with told me that, to ensure a broad range of candidates is considered for a given position, she required every job opening to have a diverse slate of qualified candidates *before* they went forward with any single candidate in the interview process. That way, the company made sure that no candidate was unfairly moving ahead.

Expand your social circles. In her book *The 7 Simple Habits of Inclusive Leaders*, author Melissa Majors reminds us that inclusive leaders recognize the influence their social circles may have over their viewpoints. Are your social circles all of the same race, gender, ethnicity, economic class and sexual orientation? If the majority of your social circles look and think similarly, then you likely have blind spots in regard to the experiences of others. If that is the case, acknowledge it, expand your circles and work on being open to the validity of others' experiences, even if it challenges your closely held beliefs.

Notice who is *not* speaking during a meeting. Oftentimes, one or two voices will dominate a conversation. This makes it hard for others to contribute. In a group discussion, intentionally involve everyone, especially the less vocal. You can encourage contrarian ideas by asking, "Why will this idea *not* work?"

2

A Desire to Belong

I T WAS 2001, and it had been one year since Alexandra Navarro arrived in Florida from South America. She had earned her BA in engineering from Universidad de la Sabana in Bogota, Colombia, and had worked in her native country as an engineer for six years. The work culture there for professional women was challenging, to say the least, so she moved to the United States to search for a better environment. However, when she arrived in the U.S., her engineering degree was not transferable, and she came to the realization that she had to begin at the bottom.

Despite being an engineer, Alexandra had to start all over. She began selling flowers, earrings, anything to make a living. She quickly learned that in Miami, Florida, appearances mattered. Fashion was important and so was the car you drove. Even if you were not rich, you had to act like you were, so she used all her money to buy nice clothes and shoes and, when she had earned enough, a new car. This, she thought, would be her ticket to acceptance in her new job. She had been hired as a business account analyst for a leading multinational importer and distributor of fresh-cut flowers. She believed that her shiny new green Geo Metro would impress the office.

Alexandra was so proud of her Geo Metro. Before buying it, she had needed to endure a treacherous commute to get to work: she would routinely take two to three buses, which also included a forty-five-minute walk to get from the first bus to the second. This was also Miami in the summer—hot and humid— so Alexandra would often need to "freshen up" by running under some sprinklers she regularly passed by during her slog to the office. After a rash on her skin appeared, she realized these "sprinklers" were actually recycled waste. To say that she was excited about that new Geo Metro (which had air conditioning!) is an understatement. The car was also exactly the same as one she had back in Colombia, where it was considered "a really cool car," so she was looking forward to showing up to work with it. So, on a hot Florida summer day, she proudly drove that new green Geo Metro to her job.

A few hours after she arrived in the office, she overheard the president's executive assistant say to her co-workers, "Did you see the ugly, crappy car that Alexandra drove in with today? Not even my housekeeper has that kind of car."

Everybody laughed.

Alexandra stood frozen in silence.

The parking lot was filled with luxury cars—Mercedes-Benz, Porsche, BMW—and the Geo Metro did not make the cut. A whirlwind of embarrassment filled her body and she immediately ran out of the room, hurried into the bathroom and started crying. She had worked so desperately to belong, to fit into the trendy lifestyles of the Floridian culture, but she could not.

In that moment, Alexandra's best was not good enough. As you will learn later in this book, Alexandra went through her own personal transformation and is now shining in her new role. But it was a long journey for her.

I met Alexandra during my time at Looker. At the time, she was working for a non-profit organization helping the Latino community acquire computer programming skills, and we came together to create a summer coding program for local youth. For all of us who have tried to be someone we are not, Alexandra's Geo Metro story is very familiar. For me, I was constantly trying to say the right things, look a certain way and play the proper roles. My best was often not good enough, either.

Fitting in and seeking approval were my daily activities. Get some praise for a job well done, and life was good. Fit in with the soccer moms because I wore the right outfit and had the latest handbag, and I could sleep at night. Get asked to join the other executives for a happy hour, and I felt like I made it "into the club." Like Alexandra, I wanted to fit in. I was constantly seeking the approval of my friends and colleagues. I wanted to belong.

I moved through the world trying to please others and get their acceptance. But what I didn't realize is that the world around me was constantly telling me that my authentic self was not enough. If your particular race, gender, sexual orientation or disability makes others in the room feel uncomfortable, then how are you supposed to show up as your authentic self and how are you expected to get the approval that you are so desperately seeking? I didn't realize that I was swimming against a current that was pulling me under with each attempt to fit in.

Messages from the Outside World Can Have a Negative Impact

In *The New Yorker*, Malcolm Gladwell once asked, "Why... do the children of recent immigrants almost never retain the accents of their parents?" There could be a number of reasons, but I would argue that it is simply the desire to belong. It is not easy being the different kid on the playground. If that difference is made fun of, you quickly learn that life is much easier if you just change that part of yourself that stands out. So, the child of the recent immigrant learns to lose her accent so that she is like the other kids.

The media, our culture and societal norms play a significant role in whether you feel like you belong. When we watch TV, do we see ourselves and our family as doctors and lawyers or as housekeepers and criminals? Sometimes there are very deliberate messages telling you that you don't belong, such as off-the-cuff remarks from friends or co-workers saying that your particular identity is "wrong," "less qualified" or simply "not normal." Other times they can be subtle, unconscious words and actions that send a signal that you don't belong, such as not getting the job because you were "just not the right cultural fit." No matter whether they are blunt and in-your-face or small unconscious jabs delivered over decades, these devaluing messages can have a devasting impact on how you view yourself, making your desire to belong even stronger.

It is hard to climb to the top when you are constantly hearing negative messages about your identity. For me, my questions over my ethnic background and whether it was "good enough" began in childhood. I grew up in a little suburb outside of Los Angeles, California. Given our close proximity to Hollywood, there were parents in our community who worked in the entertainment industry. Before I knew it, I had a talent agent and decided to give acting a shot. To this day, the idea of having an agent sounds like something out of a fairy tale, but somehow, at ten years old, I had one.

One of the first things you need is a headshot. I remember the day we took them. I carefully lined up several different outfits and we spent hours outside taking photos ranging from me standing next to a large oak tree to roller-skating down the street. It was such an exhilarating day, and I was filled with hope.

We carefully hand-picked the photos we would use and, with that, my official acting career was launched. On one side of my headshot was a full-page picture of me with my name in big letters: "TRICIA MONTALVO." On the back side were five smaller pictures of me in different angles and activities, with my name in the middle. It felt so professional and legitimate.

Auditioning for parts when you are an unknown actress is exhausting and painful. To say that learning to handle rejection is challenging is an understatement. After each submission I would wait anxiously to hear the news. I was quickly rejected before I even had an opportunity to show the casting crew that I could act.

After many months of no callbacks, my agent called up and said, "I've figured out why you're not getting any parts. *It's your last name.*"

She explained that the casting agents would likely see my Latino-sounding name on the headshot and dismiss me for any of the "American" parts. I was instantly typecast for solely Spanish-speaking parts appearing on stations such as Telemundo. She recommended that we change my last name to something more American-sounding so I would be considered for more mainstream parts.

That one simple comment when I was ten years old changed the way I viewed myself.

I remember thinking, "If my name is not American enough, then do people view me as not an American?"

Frankly, I didn't even know what "not being American enough" meant. I felt American. I was born in America. I spoke English. I lived in a middle-class neighborhood. What did they mean when they said I was not "American" enough? This didn't make sense to me.

In order to increase my chances, my talent agent suggested that I have two headshots—one for Spanish-speaking parts that had my real name, "Tricia Montalvo," and a second one that had a new, "American" name for mainstream parts: "Tricia McLaine." Looking back, I don't remember anyone asking me whether I wanted to have a different name, or whether I even liked the name McLaine. They just told me that "stage names" were common in the entertainment industry and that this simple fix would afford me new opportunities. My mom always wanted the best for me, so she quicky acquiesced to what the agent recommended—but my dad, on the other hand, was bothered.

"What is wrong with our last name?" I remember him asking me. "Are you embarrassed of it?"

I didn't have an answer. I honestly did not know what was wrong with our last name. I didn't know if we were embarrassed of it. It sure felt like we were. My father took the change in the name—*his name*—as an assault to our heritage.

So, for a brief period of my life, I walked into auditions as Tricia McLaine. And the agent was right. More opportunities came my way, and I was given auditions for mainstream parts that I had not received before. While I had some brief success with the name change, as I reflect back on this experience, it's hard not to think of the harm this must have had on my psyche as a young person who was beginning to form her identity. What the entertainment industry, the outside world, was telling me was that I was not good enough as myself. The simple fact that my parents were born in a different country meant that I did not represent what most people in the United States viewed as "American." I had to literally change my last name to be accepted.

Fast forward fifteen years and my name changed again. It was 1998 and I was getting married. I never thought twice about whether I would take my husband's name. It was just what you did, and I didn't question it. In fact, I was excited. The messages I had learned fifteen years earlier still stuck with me and the idea of legitimately having an American-sounding name felt like a good thing, like something that would benefit me. So, that year, I went from Patricia Montalvo to Tricia Timm. And with that, my Latino identity disappeared on paper again.

Changing my name allowed me to hide my ethnicity. I was no longer glaringly Latina. I remember being asked, "What are you?" Many people assumed that I was either white or European, all of which were considered a step up from being from Mexico, Central America or South America, so I didn't necessarily correct them. My ethnicity existed under the radar for much of my adult life.

To some extent we all adapt in different settings. We are more casual at home, more playful with our close friends or more professional at work. According to psychologist, author and race relations expert Dr. Beverly Tatum, trying to find common ground with others is not harmful by itself. It becomes harmful, however, if you have to deny your own sense of identity to do so. When the effort and frequency required to adapt to your environment requires you to change who you are, that is when this practice can become problematic.

The phenomenon of adjusting one's style of speech, appearance, behavior and expression to conform to a different cultural norm is commonly known as *code-switching*. I had never heard this term before I started working on this book, and it was validating to learn that there is name for how I was feeling. According to Tatum's research, when a person from a stigmatized group (race, ethnicity, language, sexual orientation and so on) is interacting with people in a non-stigmatized group, they may code-switch to play down their group membership in order to fit in and be accepted. The person sees their code-switching as important to their chances of advancing in their career or social status.

For me, I would downplay my ethnic background when necessary to belong. I don't remember choosing to do this consciously. I didn't wake up one morning and say, "I am going to downplay my ethnicity today!" It was just something I learned to do over time. All of the messages I had learned growing up gave me the feeling that my ethnicity was not valued, and I did not want to take the risk that it could jeopardize my career or my social status. So, I didn't talk about my family in Ecuador or El Salvador. I lightened and straightened my hair. I rarely spoke Spanish in public. And I stayed quiet when derogatory remarks were made about Latinos. I am not proud of any of this. In fact, I am ashamed of it. But I now understand why I was motivated to do it.

As part of an underrepresented group, I was given an impossible choice. Reading about Tatum's research, I was comforted to learn that minorities face a dilemma: "Should they suppress their cultural identity for the sake of career success? Or should they sacrifice potential career advancement for the sake of bringing their whole selves to work?"

The dominant culture is the one that imposes its values, language and ways of behaving as what is "normal." Oftentimes the dominant culture is invisible. It is just what is accepted by the majority as "better." So, those in this group don't have to change anything about themselves to fit in—they just act and behave normally, and it's accepted. It is likely why those in the prevailing culture have a harder time understanding why fitting in or having a sense of belonging is so hard for people in underrepresented groups. They have never had to expend much energy to fit in. On the other hand, those who are *not* part of the dominant culture must adapt to it or change something about themselves to fit in. This daily, hourly or even minute-by-minute process of evaluating a situation and changing how you behave in it can take a tremendous amount of energy and, after a while, it takes an emotional toll.

SELF-REFLECTION MOMENT

- Take a moment to think about whether you have ever changed anything about yourself to fit in. Make a list and examine it.

- What did you change about yourself, and how did it make you feel? Write down these feelings.

- Now, imagine what it would feel like if you didn't change to adapt to your surroundings. What would happen if you just did what came comfortably to you and didn't worry about how others reacted? How would that that feel?

The Scan-Evaluate-Adapt Process

In Chapter 1, I labeled this process of adapting to your environment as "Scan-Evaluate-Adapt." It is the exercise of carefully evaluating your surroundings and determining what it is about yourself that you need to adapt for a particular setting. It can either be a very obvious change, such as modifying your speech or hairstyle, or it can be very subtle, such as altering your mannerisms. But, either way, the cycle of Scan-Evaluate-Adapt is energy draining and anxiety producing.

Here is a good example of how I did this myself. Early in my career, I learned that I had to change my speech, style and mannerism depending on who I was talking to. If I was talking to the CEO or another executive at the company, I would stand tall and confident and talk about the economy or the latest trend in the software industry or stock market. If the executive was younger than me and male, then I would grab a beer and talk about sports. At some point in the evening I would find myself talking with a male executive's wife—who oftentimes was a stay-at-home mom, so I would switch again to soften my tone and posture and casually talk about our kids and their activities. If someone new joined the conversation and I didn't know where they fit in to this whole picture, I would stay quiet. I would listen and observe who they were and what they were about so I could decide which persona would need to show up. This would continue the whole night, back and forth, every time the audience changed. By the end of the evening, I would come home exhausted.

I switched back and forth without knowing there was an official name for what I was doing. I just instinctively knew that it was the only way to belong. In reviewing research from Pew, I learned that Black and Latino people code-switch or change their behaviors around their white colleagues. If you ask any Black or Latino person, you will find that code-switching is second nature to them. Even former President Barack Obama engages in code-switching, something that was captured in a now-famous video of his meeting with the U.S. men's Olympic basketball team. As he approached the coaches and players to shake their hands, there was a clear difference between how he greeted a white assistant coach and how he greeted Black NBA legend Kevin Durant. With the white assistant coach, it was a firm formal handshake with an air of professionalism around it, and with Durant it was a one-arm swing shake with shoulder bump like they were old friends.

Changing your physical appearance to fit in is another example of code-switching. Black women often decide to change their natural hairstyle to conform to a more traditional "Eurocentric" hairstyle for the workplace to make others feel more comfortable. In fact, I was saddened to learn that, according to a Dove CROWN research study, Black women are 80 percent more likely to change their natural hair to meet societal norms for work. Black women often change their hairstyle in this manner to avoid having to talk about their hair. Again, this takes an emotional toll over time and, in fact, denies a Black woman the opportunity to simply show up at work and do her job. Not only does she have to spend additional time worried about how her hair looks in the morning and whether it will be subject to scrutiny, her hair often becomes a topic of conversation in the workplace as well.

Code-switching can come in many different forms and can have very different impacts on a person. For some, it can be a one-time adaption that quickly becomes part of who they are without too much consternation; for others, it can be a daily or hourly chore that becomes emotionally exhausting. Why is it okay for some and not for others? Some will argue that, to some extent, we all have to adapt to our environments, and this is just part of co-existing with so many different people and cultures. While that may be true, if this behavior results in you hiding your authentic self, then this is when you start to feel the weight.

Code-switching is not always harmful. My husband, Derek, grew up in Berea, Kentucky, a small town outside of Lexington. Both of his parents were educators. He mother was an English teacher, and his father was a professor at the local university. Within his family, he grew up learning standard American English and his parents made it a point that he speak proper English when he was at home. But in his small rural community, the kids spoke in slang. He was teased if he used proper grammar at school, so he quickly learned to speak in slang on the playground: he might say "there ain't no way" instead of "there isn't any way," or "yeller jacket" instead of "yellow jacket." Then he would change to proper English when he got home to his family. As a child in Kentucky, he would spend his days switching back and forth.

In the 1980s, when he was fourteen, Derek's parents decided to move to California. In an instant, he was transported from a small rural southern town in Kentucky to a large diverse suburb in Stockton, California. He instinctively knew that he needed to speak in standard American English versus Kentucky slang in his new home, but what he didn't realize is how different and odd his accent would be.

In this new setting, he found himself in a new dilemma. His standard English was perfectly okay, but now his Southern accent was not. While the teenage girls thought it was cute, the boys certainly did not. After some rough locker-room encounters, the twang quickly disappeared and he learned to speak without his Southern accent. He settled into his new way of speaking and, with that one-time change, he could fit in. The code-switching he was forced into during his childhood was no longer necessary once he acquired an accent that was acceptable in all California settings: home, school and work. This meant he no longer had to expend any energy on adapting when he moved from one situation to another.

This unique childhood experience of having to change to fit in made Derek realize what it feels like to be an "other"—to not belong—something that has created in him a lifelong empathy for people who are different. Consequently, throughout his personal and professional life, he has been drawn to the "others" in the crowd, seeking to make them feel welcome and embracing their differences.

He was a lucky one, though. For many others, code-switching remains a treacherous daily or hourly process of modifying their authentic self. And those who engage in this "Scan-Evaluate-Adapt" process may perceive that their authentic selves are being devalued, reducing their commitment to the company and their desire to contribute their unique insights.

NEXT SMALL THING

Back on page TK, I asked you to create a list of changes you often make in order to fit in. Pick one thing from this list and, the next time that situation arises, try *not* to change it. Instead, try to show up in a way that makes you feel most comfortable. Most authentic. You can try this first in a place like a grocery store, where nobody knows you. It may feel uncomfortable at first, but try anyway. And then try it again. Each time you try it, you will start noticing that it becomes less hard.

It Is Painful to Feel Like You Don't Belong in the Room

At our core, we all want to belong. We also all want to believe that our individual success was achieved on our own merit. When we don't believe that we have succeeded on our own, we begin to question ourselves and whether we belong in the room. That is what happened to me as a result of an affirmative action program that, ironically, was designed to help me. It was an unintended consequence of a program that was meant to increase diversity and increase opportunities for traditionally marginalized groups.

Affirmative action and diversity programs seek to increase diversity in all areas of society by bringing in myriad views, perspectives and experiences that should ultimately contribute and enrich conversations. They force groups to look outside of their immediate sphere and to witness their blind spots. Studies have shown that diversity ultimately leads to better results and better profits. But not everyone agrees with this philosophy. In fact, many people argue that affirmative action is a form of reverse discrimination. All of a sudden these programs, intended to benefit society, are pitting one group against another. It has left one side feeling like their seat has been stolen by a member of an underrepresented group, and the other feeling like they don't deserve anything they accomplished because they got a perceived "leg up."

This is exactly what happened to me. I had internalized the idea that my accomplishments were solely attributed to affirmative action programs rather than merit. Sometimes I look back at that moment when I "checked the box" during my college application process and wonder whether it was worth it.

It was 1988 and it was time to fill out college applications. Since my parents had enrolled me in a college preparatory school, I was expected to go to a four-year university. I recognize that it is a privilege that I attended a private school and that I did not have the same challenges that many kids face in lower-income school districts. In fact, that privilege alone made me feel like I was unworthy of "checking the box." As we worked on our applications at school, my friends and I would talk about what school we were applying to. I was going to be a first-generation college student, so my parents couldn't help me with the application process. I relied on the academic counselor at my school for that advice. I remember sitting in her office one day and asking for her help in filling out the application.

"What should I check for the ethnicity box?"

"Where are your parents from?"

"My mom is from El Salvador and my father is from Ecuador."

"Well, that's easy, then you check the box for Hispanic."

She then moved on to the next question.

Wait. Was that the right box? Was I really Hispanic? Up to that point, I had spent so much of my life convincing myself and those around me that I was white that it didn't feel right for me to check Hispanic. Yes, it was true that my parents were first-generation immigrants from South and Central America, with deep ethnic roots in terms of both language and culture. But, by that point in my life, I was refusing to speak Spanish at home, we lived in a middle-class neighborhood and I attended a private college prep school. Because of what was engrained in me by my peers and the media, I had internalized that "Hispanic" meant you came from a low-income community, went to an under-resourced public school or needed extra help. It felt like I was somehow taking advantage of the system if I checked the Hispanic box, because I was middle-class. But the college counselor insisted that there was nothing wrong with checking that box, and that, in fact, it was the only correct box given where my parents were born. That was truly my ethnicity.

I'm not sure when and where I first heard that affirmative action wasn't fair. But it is something that has been repeated over and over again to me from the time I was applying for college, during law school in the 1990s and now as a parent of a college-bound teenager. During each phase in my life, I would inevitably hear someone say that affirmative action was a form of reverse discrimination. I would typically stay quiet when this happened for fear that, somehow, someone would find out that I had identified as Hispanic in my own school applications. I felt shame for checking that box. But there was something even deeper going on. What I didn't realize was that I actually *believed* what they were saying. I actually believed that I somehow *did* get an unfair advantage by checking the Hispanic box on those school applications. That my acceptance into college was solely due to the fact that I was Hispanic instead of my leadership, my stellar academic GPA and my strong test scores.

This belief continued as I went to law school and then throughout my career. Even though I graduated top of my class and cum laude from both college and law school, I continued to believe that I somehow got an unfair advantage. Even as I worked my way to the top of my field as general counsel, I always felt like I had to prove that I dutifully earned my spot at the table. I didn't realize that I was suffering from what I later learned is called *imposter syndrome.*

Imposter syndrome is often described as the feeling that your success is attributable to luck rather than ability. You simply cannot internalize success. This challenge is especially common for women of color. For me, imposter syndrome is very personal. When it shows up for me, it is *truth* to me. It is this feeling deep inside that you are not good enough. I can feel it throughout my body, with every muscle tied in a hard knot. And despite those around me who make the effort to remind me of what I have accomplished, I cannot shake the feeling that it was somehow luck that led to my success. Ironically, I can see others and their accomplishments very clearly, but not my own. I have suffered from imposter syndrome my entire career. It has been paralyzing at times. It has held me back from speaking up in meetings, from seeking promotions and from applying for more senior positions.

And while imposter syndrome may happen often to women and people of color, it can really happen to anyone. A study by the *Harvard Business Review* examined how the workplace environment contributes to perpetuating imposter syndrome. Authors Ruchika Tulshyan and Jodi-Ann Burey argued that while white men can certainly start their careers with imposter syndrome, as they progress through the workforce, their feelings of doubt abate as their work and intelligence are validated over time.

White men can also usually find people in leadership who look like them, and their competence or leadership style are rarely questioned. The opposite is true for women, particularly women of color. This rings true for me. Over my twenty-five-year career in law and high tech, I never saw a Latina in a position of leadership in any organization I worked for. I also never had a female manager. All of my managers were white men. This is not to say that they were not wonderful people. In fact, my managers have been some of my biggest sponsors and supporters in my career, and have greatly contributed to my success. But I never saw someone who looked like me in a leadership position, which made it hard for me to imagine that I deserved to be there. I navigated each step on the proverbial corporate ladder alone. Nobody around me was a woman, nobody around me was a Latina. Even though I was general counsel, people often confused me for the paralegal or the executive assistant, further eroding my confidence and contributing to my imposter syndrome.

I learned that I was not alone in my feelings of invisibility when I read Deepa Purushothaman's book, *The First, the Few, the Only*. In her book, Purushothaman describes the challenges that are unique to women of color in the workplace:

> Not seeing ourselves represented, or seeing ourselves represented negatively through stereotypes, affects our psyches. Without having people around us who loudly and continuously tell us that we belong, many women of color believe that we don't. That feeling runs deep and causes confusion, pain and shame... Our limited role models set us up for a life of constantly doubting our abilities, accomplishments and opportunities.

Consider the messages you have received in your life from your family, religion, media or culture that may have contributed to you thinking you are different or "not normal." Examine this list of images, stories or messages and reflect on how they may have impacted the way you see yourself. Think about who you see in roles of leadership or authority and those you see in roles of administrative work or service. One year, I was invited to attend a board dinner at CordeValle, a luxury golf resort located in Northern California that happens to be nestled right next to a predominantly Latino community. As I walked to my dinner table, I looked around and realized that all of the waiters, bussers and service staff were Latino and all of the guests, including everyone I was with, were white. I remember asking myself: *Where do I belong?*

The Third Space

For most of my life I felt like I didn't belong anywhere. I wasn't white enough to fit into the mainstream spaces or brown enough to belong in Latino spaces. I always thought of this as a disadvantage, but what if it is actually a gift?

A few years ago, I attended an event sponsored by HOPE (Hispanas Organized for Political Equality). I had been asked to speak on Latina entrepreneurship, and I was excited to share what I had learned about venture capital, network with Latina entrepreneurs and encourage more Latinas to become investors. As I walked into the room to grab breakfast before the keynote, I paused and looked around. Something was different. Everywhere I looked there were only Latinas. Young. Old. Curly brown hair. Bright colored clothing. Many were speaking Spanish. I saw hugs between old friends who hadn't seen each other in years. I saw young professionals eager to start their careers and I witnessed seasoned trailblazers sharing their wisdom with the next generation. Eight hundred Latinas together in one single room.

In that split second, it dawned on me what was different. I had never attended a corporate event where *everyone* looked like me. I had never stood in a room where the people around me shared similar life experiences. As each speaker took the stage, they joked of gossiping with their tías, of the meals carefully prepared by their mamás and of the tenderness of their abuelita's hug and we all shared a collective smile. My body was relaxed as I listened to their stories because they were also my stories. But while I felt like these were my people, I also felt like I didn't belong. I felt like a fraud. *Do I deserve to be in this room? Am I brown enough to belong here?*

On the opposite end of this thought spectrum was whether I was white enough to belong in most of the spaces I had occupied my whole life. Most of my friends were white. I lived in a predominantly white community. I was usually the only woman of color in the workplace. My lighter skin had given me access to these spaces but I never felt quite at home. My lived experience was very different from those around me. I felt pretty lonely.

So, where do I belong?

I learned that this feeling of not feeling like you belong with either identity is called *racial imposter syndrome*. This is the feeling of self-doubt when a person's internal racial identity doesn't match others' perception of their racial identity, or the feeling when a multiracial/mixed person doesn't believe they belong to any part of their racial identity. This feeling can make it hard for individuals to connect and engage with the communities with which they identify. This can happen often with multiracial and multi-ethnic and bicultural people, especially if someone loses their family language. But, as have I explained, it also happened to me even though both of my parents were Latino and my first language was Spanish. I struggled in identifying with either identity because I was forced to assimilate at such a young age.

The same was the case for thirty-one-year-old sales account executive Jaleel Mackey. We will learn more about his struggle with mental health in Chapter 3, but the first thing you need to know about Jaleel is that he is the son of an interracial couple.

His dad is Black and his mother is white. As he described to me when I interviewed him, Jaleel recalls that on his father's side he was never Black enough and on his mother's side he was too Black. His grandfather on his mother's side disowned him because he was half Black and Jaleel has only spoken to him once in his life. On his father's side, he was always trying to accentuate his Blackness in order to be Black enough to fit in with his cousins. Jaleel never felt like he belonged on either side of the family.

Dr. Sarah Gaither, a psychologist who runs the Identity and Diversity Lab at Duke University, is biracial and calls herself a me-searcher. Her work focuses on why it is so hard for multiracial and biracial people to develop a real sense of belonging. She explored this question in an NPR podcast:

> We all want to belong to certain groups. And when a mixed-race person is constantly struggling across every context of their life to be white enough or black enough or Asian enough or Latino enough, that creates a sense of imposter syndrome or this extra need to try and belong to these groups. Being constantly told that you never fit in to your respective racial backgrounds really does make you feel like a fake person. It makes you feel like you don't have a family, you don't have a group to call your own.

I was not surprised to learn that Gaither's research found that multiracial people tend to face the highest levels of social exclusion as compared to other racial or ethnic groups. In fact, she found that they are excluded twice as often. This often leads to a higher incidence of mental health conditions, since they are constantly trying to fit in. This was certainly the case for Jaleel.

So, when you find yourself in this situation, how do you move from a feeling of exclusion to a feeling of inclusion?

One way is to start believing that you have the right to claim *both* as your identity. You are not too white and don't need to speak Spanish in order to be Latino. You don't have to be born in Asia to be Asian. And you don't have to have dark black skin and kinky hair to be Black. In fact, Jaleel describes his hair as a true embodiment of his biracial identity. He has curly black hair, but it is long with soft waves and not kinky. He did not mean to grow out his hair at first, but as it grew long and wavy, he saw the combination of his two identities literally embodied in his hair. It gave him the opportunity to reconnect with that part of himself. Jaleel started to begin to accept both of his identities.

While there is no doubt that it is a struggle to feel like you belong in either space, I also see it as an opportunity. Being able to occupy both spaces gives you the ability to see the perspective from both sides. Jaleel calls this "the third space." For those of you who have straddled two racial identities, the third space comes with the privilege of access to conversations that you would not otherwise have access to if you were exclusively labeled as one identity. In Jaleel's case, he found himself in conversations that he would not be privy to if his skin were darker as well as in conversations that he would not be privy to if his skin were lighter. He is accepted in more circles because he doesn't fit into a single box. I find the same to be true for me. I often find myself in conversations where I have the opportunity to provide a different perspective than is present because I was invited into that room. Here is what Jaleel had to say about being biracial:

> I am man of the people. I am a human being and connected
> to more than I can even imagine. It is both a gift and curse.
> I also have the responsibility of healing the racial traumas

that I am carrying in this body. I am carrying hundreds of years of racial trauma in this Black body. I am also carrying hundreds of years of racial oppression that I have experienced and exerted on other beings in this body. I am in the process of healing both.

Being biracial or suffering racial imposter syndrome is very difficult. You may often feel like you don't belong anywhere. But if you can find a way to embrace both identities, it may actually give you a unique lens you didn't know you had. That doesn't mean that at times it won't get emotionally exhausting to be the only one in the room, so we'll explore when to choose self-care in Chapter 7.

Self-Acceptance Is the First Step

From changing my name to code-switching to the impact of affirmative action, my life experiences had me questioning whether I belonged in the room. I spent many years feeling angry and frustrated with everyone and everything around me. I blamed others for my sense that I did not belong. I pointed fingers, saying that others had forced me to change in order to fit in and that it all wasn't fair. I would say to myself, "If everybody would just accept me, then everything would be okay." What I didn't ask myself was this: *How can anyone accept me if I don't accept myself first?* If I believed I was enough, then others would as well.

Belonging begins with self-acceptance.

Accepting yourself when you've had years or decades of messages telling you that you are unworthy takes some time to unpack. For those in underrepresented groups, this can be incredibly hard because the outside world has constantly sent you messages that you do not in fact belong. But it has to begin with you. You have to begin the healing process by unpacking these messages that told you that you were unworthy.

Once I started showing up as my true self, opportunities began to open up. When I decided that the only way to show up was to simply be myself, that is when I was freed.

Throughout this book, I share some of the ways you can begin unpacking these emotions and get on the road to self-acceptance. My hope for you is that, by the end of the book, you will feel seen, embrace what makes you unique and understand how it brings value to an organization.

You may be thinking to yourself, "Will this feeling of being an outsider ever go away? Will I ever feel like I belong?"

I think the answer is both yes and no. While it may seem impossible in this moment to believe that you can ever feel like you belong in the room, I can assure you that, through some self-reflection, support and practice, you can absolutely get to that place. As you grow in confidence in yourself, that feeling of inadequacy will slowly dissipate. You may not notice it at first, but then one day you realize you didn't change a thing about yourself and everything is fine. When you get to that place, that is when you will thrive. You will not only feel like you *belong* in the room, you will have so much confidence in yourself that you will *own* the room.

On the other hand, even if you get this confidence in one particular environment or moment, you might enter a new environment and find that all of those old feelings of inadequacies are rushing back. Maybe it's a new job, promotion or stretch project. But this time around, you will have the tools to recognize it and chip away at those feelings.

You can do this.

MANAGER STRATEGIES

If you want your employees to have a sense of belonging at work, you have to be proactive about creating an inclusive environment. One place to start is by examining your own biases and how you may be unintentionally "othering" your employees at work.

Develop an inclusion mindset. Author Ruchika Tulshyan tells us that inclusion isn't an inborn trait. It takes awareness, intention and regular practice. She has created a memorable acronym—BRIDGE—to approach cultivating an inclusion mindset for leaders:

- Be uncomfortable.
- Reflect (on what you don't know).
- Invite feedback.
- Defensiveness doesn't help.
- Grow from your mistakes.
- Expect that change takes time.

Conduct unconscious bias training at your company. Many times, people do not know that the things they say or do are harming another person. The first step is to educate your employees about unconscious bias. Consider conducting company-wide unconscious bias training so that employees can begin the journey of becoming more aware of their personal biases and belief systems.

Don't call it a "diversity hire" or "diversity quota." This will backfire on you. If your employees are feeling like they were hired to simply "check the box" they will not have a sense of belonging. Characterizing recruiting in this manner also undermines the skills and qualifications of a diverse candidate when they join the organization. Right from the start, they will feel like they have to hustle a little bit harder to prove they belong in the room. Instead, frame your recruiting efforts like this: You want to hire the most qualified person for the position—who is also diverse, making them even more qualified because of their unique perspective. Make it clear that you are not lowering your standards.

Don't "other" your diverse employees. With the pressure to diversify the workforce, many companies are updating their website to showcase their latest DEI efforts. That is good, until you start asking your very few diverse employees to pose for pictures for the corporate website. This makes your diverse employees feel used and further highlights their "otherness." And if your company is not diverse and has a long way to go, be honest about where you are at on DEI as a company and commit to doing better.

3

Hiding in Plain Sight

EING AN OUTSIDER is not easy. Many of us learned this tough lesson in middle school. Sometimes the desire to belong is so strong that we are willing to do whatever it takes to fit in, including holding parts of ourselves back. There are people from many groups who will be familiar with the act of hiding a piece of your identity. We have seen this in the LGBTQ+ community, where some people may choose not to reveal their sexual orientation or gender identity in order to make others around them feel comfortable. We have also seen generations of people keep their religious affiliation a secret, particularly those who may be under political attack, such as those in the Jewish or Muslim communities. The same is true in the Latino community where, if you have light skin, do not have an accent and your last name does not sound ethnic, you can often pass as white or European. For many in this group, covering their ethnicity has been essential to progressing in the workforce. That was the case for me.

The idea of hiding came from my mom, or, as I call her, Mami. She simply wanted to protect me, and her advice came from a place of love. My mother had a heavy accent and was not able to easily hide her background. El Salvador was also immersed in a civil war, so there was a lot of negative press in the media about this beautiful country. As a result, my mother experienced discrimination and wanted to spare me from that pain.

I remember her once telling me a story about being denied equal pay.

"I asked my boss one day why I wasn't getting paid the same as a man who held the same job," Mami said. "He told me that, unfortunately, this the way it is for 'people like me' and that I 'just had to get over it' as I would not get a job like this anywhere else. So I just needed to live with it."

I was shocked that a manager could be so outwardly discriminatory to my mom. "Why didn't you just leave that job?" I asked.

"No, Patita," she told me. "He was right. It would be very hard for me to get another job like this, so I just had to accept it."

Yet, Mami was a fighter. Despite all odds, she rose through the ranks to become branch manager at our local bank, but not without having to overcome many obstacles along the way. To spare me that discomfort, she suggested that life would be much easier if I simply did not reveal where I was from. She was a mother who didn't want to see her daughter experience the same pain from discrimination that she had endured. But, for me, decades of hiding my authentic self took its toll.

Passing as White

Throughout my career, I hid two main parts of my life: my ethnicity and my role as a mom. I was convinced that neither identity would serve me well in the corporate world. I was focused on being successful in my career and making it to the top, so hiding these parts of myself was a price I was willing to pay.

At work, I was able to pass as white. After I married my name changed to Tricia Timm, so my Latino roots became invisible. I straightened my hair, wore the proper clothes and said the right things. Being a part of the mainstream was seemingly easy. You simply go along with what everyone else is saying and doing. It felt like there was not much damage that could be created from that. Or so I thought.

What I did not yet appreciate was what happens to you when what everyone else is doing or saying contradicts with your core values.

I remember sitting in on one of my client's board meetings. I was the only woman and only person of color in the room, but I was pretty accustomed to this by that point in my career. I was also the youngest person in the room. I was taking the minutes, so I felt more like a scribe than a participant. I had taken a seat at the end of a long table and left several seats open between me and the next person. I'm not sure anyone even noticed I was there.

During one of the breaks, we got up to grab some snacks and the group got engrossed in small talk. It was an election year. I expected to hear political positions that I didn't agree with, but I did not expect to hear the following from one of the directors:

"The problem is that too many uneducated people have the right to vote. We really need to go back to the days when only landowners could vote. That would be much better."

I sat there, stunned. *Did he just say that?*

I looked around to see if there were any other surprised faces in the room. I expected to see at least one person as bothered by that comment as I was. But nothing. Some of the other directors nodded their heads in agreement, others continued eating their snacks and the conversation continued.

In an instant, I felt disconnected from the group. I didn't have the statistics in front of me, but I felt pretty confident that limiting the right to vote to only landowners would largely impact underrepresented or lower-income groups. I was a young lawyer at the time, so I did not feel like I could speak up in that moment, so I stayed quiet and distraught. I did not want to put my job or credibility on the line by disagreeing with a board member, so I had no choice but to brush off this comment and stay silent. Like my mom before me, I thought: *I have no choice. I need this job, so I just have to accept it.* So I did.

Keeping my opinion to myself in that moment felt like the only thing I could do. But, in retrospect, what a disservice that was to everyone in that organization whose rights were being so casually tossed aside by the board members in that room. So many employees at that company did not own land—many of them people of color. By keeping my thoughts to myself and not sharing a different point of view, I allowed bias to continue at the highest corporate levels.

The Invisible Family

There was another aspect of my identity I felt I needed to hide as I climbed the corporate ladder: the role of a new parent. The news of my pregnancy shocked my boss and, as a result, when I returned from maternity leave I pretended that I did not have a newborn at home. I kept my family life separate from my work life. I kept my new family invisible.

It was 2002 and I was the second in command in the legal department at a publicly traded company. I was about six years into being a lawyer, so this was an important role for me. It was a very demanding job with tremendous responsibility. My boss at the time was a single man, and he worked 24/7. Since I was a quick learner and hard worker, he began to give me a lot of responsibility. Soon, he began to rely on me for most things. When I decided to start a family, I was terrified to tell him of my pregnancy. At the time, there were no other women in leadership or any parent support groups, so there was no one to give advice on how to manage a pregnancy at work, let alone how to navigate maternity leave and the transition back. There was no guidebook on how I could pull this off successfully.

Not seeing any female leaders at my company that were either pregnant or balancing a family made it hard for me to feel like I could succeed as a working mom. I also didn't see many dads at work. Of course, there were plenty of men in the office who were fathers, but I rarely saw them "show up" as dads. I didn't hear much of their families. I didn't see or notice any men leaving early to catch a baseball game or dance recital, and there were certainly no men at that time who were taking paternity leave. It was like families were invisible. This was pre-social media and we only saw our co-workers' families once a year, at the annual family BBQ.

As my due date crept closer and closer, I couldn't hide my emerging belly. I dreaded the day that I had to tell my boss I was pregnant. I knew he would not take it well. I wish I could tell you that things went swimmingly. That he was overjoyed at my pregnancy and the fact that I was about to embark on one of the most amazing chapters of my life—being a new mom!

At first, his reaction was dead silence. My heart felt like it was beating outside of my chest as I anticipated what he would say.

Then he asked, "How could you do this to me?"

I just stood there, shocked, not knowing how to respond.

We remained in dead silence for what felt like hours but was probably only a few minutes. He then simply looked at me and said, "I've seen this movie; I know how it ends." And then he walked away.

I took this to mean that he believed I would either not return to work or would somehow deprioritize my career and drop out of the workforce. In any event, my status in his eyes changed in that split second. I suspected that any chance of a promotion after this was over.

My heart sank and I felt like I had let down my father in that moment. A boss who had advocated for me in the past was acting as if I had betrayed him, as though I had abandoned him just when he needed me most. Instead of feelings of joy and excitement in sharing the news of my pregnancy, I experienced a tremendous sense of guilt for letting him down.

While I had to endure days of the silent treatment, the news eventually sunk in and my boss and I started working together on a transition plan for my three-month maternity leave. Going out on leave was hard but returning to work was even harder. Co-workers constantly asked whether I would return to work, and people assumed that I would be less accessible once I had my daughter.

Many times I wanted to quit this job. To leave it and this environment altogether. However, I was about to have a baby, I was the sole breadwinner at the time, and nobody would hire a pregnant woman (or so I thought), so I needed to stay. But I think that, subconsciously, this was the beginning of the end of my loyalty at that company. While I ended up staying for a couple more years, it was through sheer grit that I got through it. I decided to focus on the experience and skills I was gaining, but I did not enjoy my job. As a result, my husband and I started thinking about changes we could make in our lives that would allow me to eventually leave that company.

Despite my resolve that life would not change when our baby was born, like every for new parent, our life *did* in fact change. Before having kids, I could work all day without interruption, work late if needed, sleep a full night, catch up with errands and, more importantly, rest on the weekends. Once you have kids, this all changes.

For me, things were exacerbated more because my daughter initially refused to take a bottle and so, for my first few months back at work, I had to nurse her during the workday. In an instant, I had to figure out a way to nurse my baby every three hours without disrupting my schedule. And, I had to find a subtle way for my husband to bring her to the office so I could feed her without bringing too much attention to it. Luckily, I had my own office and could shut my door and nurse her. But what would I do if I had to attend an offsite meeting?

These were the days before Zoom meetings and "flex schedules." I had to be in the office for at least eight hours every day, in person. Period. It was up to me to figure out how to fit my new life as a working parent into this structured workday. My husband and I decided that the only way we could do this was for him to drive to wherever I was having my meeting, then I would sneak away during a break and nurse my baby in the parking garage. Since I was already feeling the immense fear that I would no longer be respected at my job, I did this very discreetly. I didn't want to be excluded from any important meetings and I also didn't want to appear to be putting my family ahead of my career. So, I carried on like this and hid our "nursing encounters in the garage" for months until she took the bottle.

Like all new parents, I wasn't getting any sleep. I didn't have anyone at my company I could get advice from, so I felt very alone. Flextime was nonexistent and there was an expectation that I would work the same hours I had done prior to having the baby. I had to keep up that same demanding schedule to stay in the game. I felt that the only way I could do this was by hiding the struggle of being a new parent.

For many working moms, this story will be familiar. Elena Donio, a C-suite executive and board member who you will hear more about later, shared a similar experience with me. She told me how her baby also didn't take the bottle and how she would have to make an excuse as to why she had to leave in the middle of the day. She would rush over to her son's daycare to nurse, sobbing the whole way there and back. Then, upon arrival back at work, she would quickly wipe away her tears, freshen her make-up and walk back into the building as if nothing had just happened.

For many caregivers, keeping their family invisible is a common strategy. Sometimes you may be the sole breadwinner and you have to ensure you have a job when you return to work. In other cases, caregivers want to prove to their organizations that they are not choosing family over work. Whatever the reason, feeling like you have to keep your family situation a secret is a heavy burden. And this extends beyond working mothers. There are parents of disabled children who have the extra job of attending to the special needs of their child while battling the department of education or insurance companies to ensure their kids get the therapies and treatments they require. Single parents who have the weight of the world on their shoulders as they try to make sure their children are getting everything they need. Couples who are trying to start a family but are suffering silently through miscarriages and failed infertility attempts. And those who are caring for a family member who is aging or in declining health.

In all of these cases, keeping your family situation a secret comes at a cost. If you can't share with your co-workers the joys and heartaches of your family, you lose community. If there is no one around you who understands what it feels like to leave your newborn with strangers at daycare, you feel alone. If you can't share your grief when you lose a loved one, you detach.

Keeping such a special part of your life—your family—a secret results in you being disengaged with your employer. Slowly, you become more unhappy, more unfulfilled and less energized about going to work as you feel less and less supported. I kept up this charade until I could not tolerate it any longer. I left that job shortly after the birth of my second daughter.

Hiding Can Include Omitting a Part of Yourself

Hiding doesn't always mean not actively sharing a part of yourself. It can also mean quietly omitting it from the conversation.

When it came time for me to join the workforce, I decided to heed my mom's advice and keep my ethnicity out of the conversation as much as I could. I rarely talked about where my family came from. I didn't talk much about the rich history of their background, including the thirty or so aunts, uncles and cousins living in Ecuador and El Salvador who were as fun and loud as me. I also didn't talk about how my parents came to this country as immigrants and what they had to do to make it in the United States, including having two or three jobs to survive. I never spoke Spanish at work, and I didn't talk about how my mom loved mariachis, tamales and pupusas. These things stayed at home. They were not shared at work. I couldn't imagine anyone at work having so many relatives in Latin American countries or that their parents loved listening to mariachis on vacation, so I decided it was not worth the risk to reveal it. I didn't want to look at blank stares. To me, it felt like there was only downside to exposing this part of my identity, not upside. I had never heard anyone else talk about their Latino families or traditions and we had never celebrated Latino culture at work, so it seemed like that part of me didn't belong there.

At my first job at the law firm, there were many social cues I had to learn quickly. Once thing was my taste in food. When I was growing up, my parents made the decision that all their extra income would go to housing and a good education, not to fancy meals. As a result, we only went out to dinner as a family four times a year—once for each of our birthdays—and that usually ended up being at our favorite Mexican restaurant. My mom was the cook at home and also worked full-time, so her survival technique was to cook all of the week's meals on

Sunday and warm them up for us during the week. That meant we had virtually the same five meals every week for my whole childhood. Exotic cuisines or elaborate meals were not part of my life growing up. This did not serve me well as a new corporate lawyer in a large elite law firm where going out for business lunches was the norm. It may not seem like a big deal, but for me it felt like it was.

When I first started at that firm, we would often go out to lunch as a team. We would pile in someone's car and do the ten-minute drive into Palo Alto.

"Where should we go to lunch today?"

"How about sushi?"

"How about Thai?"

"How about MacArthur Park?"

I remember my body starting to tense at the suggestion of MacArthur Park. This was a well-known restaurant situated in a landmark building that served American cuisine. The last time we went there, the group had ordered popcorn shrimp and some sort of brie or goat cheese appetizer that nearly made me vomit. I started praying silently that the group would consider other options, yet sat in fear at what the next suggestion would be.

As we drove down the street, we saw an Olive Garden coming up on the right-hand side.

"How about Olive Garden?" someone exclaimed.

My heart felt like it was going to jump out of my body. I was ecstatic! *Finally, a restaurant that I know.* Unlimited soup, salad, breadsticks and pasta. Perfect!

Just as I was about to bellow, "Yes! Let's go to Olive Garden," everyone started laughing.

"I wouldn't be caught dead in that place," one of the attorneys said with a snicker.

"No way, that food is gross," another said.

My heart sank back down and a wave of embarrassment

filled my body. Luckily, I hadn't spoken out loud, but I remember feeling like a fish out of water. Everybody around me had such a different taste in food, and I knew immediately that the food I enjoyed was viewed unfavorably. In that moment, as a young first-year associate, I had a choice to make. I had a lot at stake and I needed to fit in.

"Yuck. Let's definitely not go there with so many great options to choose from," I said, joining the crowd.

So, that day, I ate some popcorn shrimp and brie (not much, though!). I never revealed that I had not experienced fine cuisine before joining that firm. Nobody needed to know.

Hiding What Is Going on Inside

In addition to variations based on our identities, another aspect of ourselves that we can commonly hide is the status of our mental health. According to the Centers for Disease Control and Prevention, an estimated 26 percent of adults are living with a mental health disorder in any given year, and 46 percent will have a mental health disorder over the course of their lifetime. In addition, 71 percent of adults report experiencing at least one symptom of stress, such as a headache or feeling overwhelmed or anxious. Many who suffer from a mental health condition don't seek help because of the stigma attached to it, or, if they do get treatment, they keep it hidden from the workplace. They are too worried about what others may think if they were open about their well-being. This was the case for Jaleel Mackey.

I first introduced you to Jaleel in the previous chapter, when I shared his experience in the "third space" as a biracial man. Thirty-one years old, he is currently a sales leader for a health tech company, and happily married, with a five-year-old son. He is also the co-founder of Breathe, Rise + Thrive, a company offering classes on breathwork and movement for holistic well-being. Jaleel now wakes up grateful for every day, and his life's purpose is to normalize conversations around mental health. But that was not always the case. Not too long ago, his marriage was crumbling, he was on the verge of losing his job and he was about to take his own life. Jaleel had kept the trauma of the domestic violence he had witnessed as a child a secret, hiding that part of his life from everyone. Yet, those experiences had set off a chain of events that caused further trauma, such as growing up with a father in prison and a mother struggling with alcoholism, and finding himself homeless. He had not realized that he had never truly processed what he had endured as a child.

Despite everything Jaleel had experienced in his young life, he did remarkably well under our societal standards. He got good grades, played football and got accepted to USC. Everything was lining up for him on the outside. He was the super kid that could overcome anything.

Things changed when Jaleel got to USC. He could no longer play football, something that, before this point, he had not realized was a major outlet for him. Football had given him a place to release his anger and sadness, and it had provided a sense of family that he did not otherwise have at home. Without football, and alone at USC, Jaleel suddenly found himself battling depression. He didn't want to get out of bed or go to class. He withdrew from classes because he thought a "W" was better than an "F." He didn't get a real diagnosis until his senior year in college, when a psychiatrist told him he was suffering from depression and ADHD. But Jaleel didn't want to believe it. He was so high functioning, he believed, that he couldn't be "one of those people" struggling with their mental health. He felt so stigmatized to be suffering from a mental health condition that he couldn't identify with it. It didn't feel true for him, so he refused to get help. He decided he could get through it like he did everything else.

Jaleel continued to grind through school and his bouts of depression and went on to graduate from USC. He found a great job at a high-tech company in sales and was crushing his sales quotas. Soon, he started a family of his own. Still in his twenties, everything on the outside looked like it was going great for him. Until it wasn't.

Jaleel had kept quiet about his turbulent past. He kept all of it buried. He was such a high achiever and high performer in all external aspects of his life and was so ashamed of his past and his mental health struggles that he couldn't face telling anyone about the unpleasant parts of his life.

Eventually, all of this unprocessed trauma caught up to him. He found himself in a place where he could no longer handle the combined pressure of work and being a new husband and father. His outside appearance as the up-and-coming sales leader was not matching his insides. He was terrified that people would think he was incapable or incompetent. His mental health was declining but he felt he would get fired if he talked about it, so instead he kept all of the pain and suffering inside. He was crumbling, but didn't know how to ask for help. He didn't know how to say:

"I'm struggling."

"Please help me navigate these emotions."

"I need help."

The weight of all the trauma he had buried and the pressure of his work became too much to bear. He started failing at work and his marriage began to fall apart. Despite his wife's appeals, Jaleel was refusing to seek help. Eventually, his wife decided she could not live that way anymore and told him she was leaving, and taking their son with her. Jaleel recalls lying in his bed with visions of taking his own life as the date of her departure approached.

"I couldn't unsee it," he told me. "It became a persistent thought."

He had even bought a new pair of shoes for his son, and written a love letter to say goodbye to him.

It was a foggy day in April. Jaleel's wife was planning to leave within the next few weeks. Jaleel was walking down the street on his way to take the A train to work. For whatever reason, he had a sudden moment of clarity. He looked up to the sky and thought to himself:

"Holy, shit. If I don't do something, I am going to die."

Instead of getting on the train, Jaleel immediately brought himself to an emergency mental health facility in Manhattan. He felt so ashamed, but he stayed there anyway. At first, he didn't tell anyone where he was. He didn't call his boss or his wife. People called him, and he didn't respond. People went to his apartment, but he wasn't home. The shame was so deep. For hours it seemed like he had disappeared, and everybody was looking for him.

When he finally returned home, his wife asked if he was thinking about taking his life. Jaleel simply responded, "Yes."

She immediately canceled her travel plans and stayed with him. He found a treatment facility in Florida for addiction and trauma for men. At that facility, he met men across various lifestyles and demographics: from wealthy CFOs to those who were on welfare and everything in between. Some had addictions to heroin or to prescription opioids. They all had different traumas and addictions, but they also had one thing in common: each felt shame for the secrets they had been carrying for so many years. They were terrified of what would happen if they told their truth. Things they had done to other people. Things that had been done to them. Things they felt guilty about. They all had pain and anger they wanted to express but didn't know how to do it. As odd as it may sound, for the first time in Jaleel's life, he felt like he belonged. Here is how he described his experience at the treatment facility:

> It was there where I could put down all the trauma in order to pick myself up again. It was there where I was introduced to breathwork and other modalities to process emotions. I didn't have to outpace the demons anymore. I didn't have to outrun the pain anymore. I learned that crying or being sad or angry was okay and I could process these emotions in a positive way. It was a beautiful container where I could finally discover what it meant to be human. To be human is to be a mess. It's beautiful and it's messy and half the time it doesn't make sense.

Jaleel was diagnosed with post-traumatic stress disorder. This diagnosis finally made sense to him. It provided to be the rationale for why he didn't trust people and why he had a problem with authority. It answered the question of why he felt like the world was going to come crashing down on him at any moment—it was because it actually had crashed down on him multiple times over in his life. His trauma had created an expectation that everything will fall apart, and that it was just a matter of time.

SELF-REFLECTION MOMENT

- What is unique about your life or lived experience that could be valuable in the workplace? Did you grow up in a different culture or religion? Did you come from an economically disadvantaged background? Did you or a family member struggle with a mental health condition?

- What useful insights do you have as a result of that specific lived experience?

- If you are keeping any part of your identity hidden, think about the reasons why that may be the case. What fears do you have? Are you afraid of being rejected? Are you afraid that your opinion will not be valued? Just notice the fears, without judgment.

Modifying Who You Are Can Achieve Real Results—at a Cost

Like Jaleel, I too hid or omitted many parts of my life in order to succeed at work. I have felt shame for hiding my Latina identity to progress in my career, and I have felt as if I was letting down my whole Latino community. I was surprised to learn that I was not alone. According to a study of Latinos at work by the think tank Coqual, the phenomenon of covering or downplaying your ethnicity to climb up the corporate ladder is quite common. In the study, 76 percent of Latinos stated that they repressed parts of their persona in the workplace, including covering or downplaying who they are, or modifying their appearance, body language or communication style.

Why do so many Latinos do this? Unfortunately, because it actually produces results. Modifying these aspects of a Latino identity—in other words, "passing as white"—has been shown to enhance a Latino's prospects of progression to management. While this might seem worth it at first glance, studies also show that taking this step can have devasting effects, not only for the individual, but for the organization as well.

A Unique Voice Can Impact Branding Campaigns

When employees do not show up comfortably and authentically at work, it deprives an organization of the opportunity to hear a different or unique perspective that could have been incredibly valuable to solving problems and to the success of the business. In the Coqual study, researchers Noni Allwood and Laura Sherbin discuss a 2010 branding campaign that was conducted by Clorox. The company had decided to commission a study to better understand the housekeeping lessons and routines of Latinas. When the study was completed, Clorox published the results on its website, writing that "cleaning was a rite of passage, taught by [Latino] mothers and grandmothers" and "cleaning is a labor of love that inspires a sense of pride."

While Clorox was well-intentioned in its study, the response from the Latino community was not what they expected. Instead of praise for their focus on the Latino community, the company received backlash for perpetuating the stereotype of Latinas as housecleaners or maids. One commentor stated, "Clorox: Brown people, make things whiter!"

So, where did Clorox go wrong?

Lack of representation. Nobody was in the room to question how this campaign would land with the Latino community. Consider how different the campaign might have looked had there been input from a Latina who felt fully seen and respected at her organization. She may have expressed her concern about perpetuating the stereotype of Latinas as maids or housekeepers and suggested a different approach. Assuming that the leaders had listened to her, this might have saved Clorox from a massive branding blunder.

These are the types of lost opportunities that companies miss out on when they don't have that unique perspective as part of the discussion. In contrast, an initiative at *Time* magazine shows the beneficial effect that inclusion can have on a campaign. When the media giant decided to launch *People en Español* magazine back in 2010, executives at the company had initially decided to simply translate the original magazine into Spanish. However, Lisa Garcia Quiroz was there to question this. Quiroz was an American business executive at Time Warner who oversaw its charitable foundation and philanthropic and corporate responsibility departments and served as its first chief diversity officer. She knew the *People en Español* launch strategy would not be successful if it was simply a translated version, as most Latinos were bilingual so they could get the same content from the U.S. version. And those who didn't speak English would likely follow different celebrities from those who were featured in the mainstream publication. So, instead, she proposed launching a different magazine that was tailored to the Latino culture and community and that would provide content they would embrace. It was a huge success.

Repressing Who You Are to "Fit In" Does Not Pay the Dividends You Think It Will

Keeping something about yourself hidden from those around you prevents you from sharing the best parts of yourself with the world. You not only deprive those around you of some of the most interesting and unique parts of yourself, you also put yourself at risk of having to engage in situations where you feel pressured to go against your beliefs.

In an episode of an NPR podcast called *Rough Translation*, the host recounts a story of an Orthodox Jewish person at work. She was afraid to tell her co-workers of her religious beliefs for fear of discrimination, so she simply did not mention it. As part of her religion, she followed the laws of negiah, which means touch. Orthodox men and women do not engage in physical contact with those of the opposite sex, outside of their spouse or immediate family members. This meant that she could not shake hands with her co-workers or when meeting new people. People thought she was being rude, but the reality was that she was simply following her religious beliefs. She eventually decided to start shaking hands so that she was not viewed poorly by others. However, with every handshake, she felt shame and guilt. Eventually, the toll was too heavy and she left.

When she started her new job, she decided to reveal her religious beliefs. To her surprise, it was welcomed. She wore her traditional dress and followed her beliefs on touch. This allowed her to contribute to the organization rather than worrying about whether or not she needed to shake hands. By showing up as her whole self, she also brought awareness about a religion many may not have known much about before. Her decision helped create empathy for others like her in the future.

NEXT SMALL THING

Do one small thing that communicates to the world what is different about you. Make a post about a holiday you are celebrating. Put up a picture at your desk of your same-sex partner. Wear a pink ribbon during Breast Cancer Awareness Month. Do some small thing that may spark someone else to ask about it. For example, when I make a post about my mom or dad on social media, I now try to include a sentence in Spanish. Let others start seeing the real you.

The Impact of Microaggressions

Another tragic result of hiding your identity is that people lose their filter around you. For me, perhaps because people believed I was white, they felt free to air their frustrations with the latest political beliefs around immigration, with the increase of Latinos in their community or this country or what they perceived as unfair government support going to low-income Latino communities. Some of these moments were overt, but many were subtle. With every slight or roll of the eyes, a little bit of me was harmed.

These subtle jabs are called *microaggressions*. Microaggressions are the small, everyday insults experienced by a marginalized group. They can be comments, actions or even just a look someone gives you. They're usually rooted in stereotypes, racist beliefs or ignorance. Microaggressions can be malicious or completely unintentional. Sometimes it might be easy to brush them off. Other times they can shake you to your core. For me, staying quiet over all those years of experiencing microaggression after microaggression created deeper and deeper wounds that I didn't even realize were happening.

Responding to microaggressions can be empowering but, if you are from a marginalized identity, you may find yourself responding to them all day long. This will eventually take a toll on you. So, the first thing you need to decide is whether or not to respond at all. In an interview with the *New York Times*, psychology professor Kevin Nadal described five questions he developed to help people weigh the consequences of responding to a microaggression. The questions are:

- "If I respond, could my physical safety be in danger?"

- "If I respond, will the person become defensive and will this lead to an argument?"

- "If I respond, how will this affect my relationship with this person?" (For example, a co-worker or family member.)

- "If I don't respond, will I regret not saying something?"

- "If I don't respond, does that convey that I accept the behavior or statement?"

As you consider these questions, think about your intended goal in responding to the microaggression. Do you want to be seen and heard? Do you want to educate? Then, if you do make the decision to respond, Nadal suggests taking three actions first:

Ask for more clarification: "Could you say more about what you mean by that?" "How have you come to think that?"

Separate intent from impact: "I know you didn't realize this, but when you _____ (comment/behavior), it was hurtful/offensive because _____. Instead you could _____ (different language or behavior)."

Share your own process: "I noticed that you _____ (comment/behavior). I used to do/say that too, but then I learned _____."

Nadal suggests that the main goal of your response should be to help the aggressor understand that they are not under attack. If we want people to truly hear what we are saying and start changing their behavior, they cannot feel defensive. If they are trying to defend their statement or behavior, they will not change.

In order to be able to respond to microaggressions, you first need to make a plan. Think about the common types of micro-aggressions you experience and ask yourself the five questions suggested by Nadal. Then, consider how you will respond the next time. Be intentional on what you would say. Write it down. You can start by using Nadal's proposed initial responses. Sometimes, the microaggression may happen so fast that you won't have time to interrupt it, and that's okay. That is why you need to prepare in advance.

Once you start interrupting microaggressions, don't feel compelled to do it all the time. Remember that self-care is vital and battling every instance is not worth it. Choose the moments that matter to you the most.

Feelings of Shame, Guilt and Loss of Identity

As I look back at my life, I have a sense of guilt and shame for all the times I did not speak up. One of the hardest moments in my life happened during a visit with some old friends.

It was a cold fall day, and we were all excited to be warming up inside the house. Our kids were school age, and the toddlers were on the floor playing.

"I am so tired of all these Hispanic people coming here and taking our jobs. I wish they would just stay in their country. I don't even see any white people at Walmart anymore," our friend casually stated.

My husband and I were sitting across from each other when we heard those words. It was clear to us that they did not realize they were talking about me. We immediately locked eyes, each of us wondering what to do next. I played out in my mind what I could say in response:

"I just want to let you know that those kinds of statements are hurtful as I am Latina and my parents were immigrants to this country."

But I didn't say it. I wanted to keep drama at a minimum.

I didn't have the language or the tools to carefully manage that conversation other than explaining that those statements were offensive, which would surely escalate things. So, I stayed quiet. I decided that I didn't want to "ruin" this special time together by challenging these statements.

I stayed quiet and these sorts of comments continued for the rest of our visit. I stayed quiet in front of my husband. I stayed quiet in front of my kids. I stayed quiet in front of all of our friends. And while things continued to be perfectly normal for everyone else in the room, my heart was crushed with each statement. I was not only upset because of the hurtful comments that were being made about the Latino community, I was also ashamed that I did not have the courage to speak up against them.

I had a similar moment with a co-worker. He was telling me how unhappy he was with a recent school program that was intended to support kids from low-income communities.

"All the Hispanic kids were getting free shoes at my school but not the white kids. Can you believe that? What about my kid? We would love to have free shoes. Why do the Hispanic kids get all the free stuff? They probably don't even pay taxes."

I'm not sure what the program was or why his kid was not getting free shoes, but he told me this story clearly assuming that I was white and that I would be equally in shock at this seemingly unfair shoe program. Again, I was confronted with that moment of whether or not I should say anything.

Do I tell him I am Latina?

Do I try to explain the topics of systemic racism and white privilege?

Do I simply offer him twenty bucks to get some free shoes for his kid?

All of these thoughts raced through my mind in a matter of seconds. The moment was pleasant, we were having a nice lunch and I questioned whether this was the right moment to confront him. I decided to stay quiet to keep things comfortable for everyone but me.

The decision to stay quiet or to embark in a difficult conversation around race is a personal one. While it is easy to say that we should confront each of those situations head on, I don't think it is that simple.

As I will discuss later in this book, part of the journey is having the tools that will help you know when and how to tackle these difficult conversations and when it is time to do a little self-care. This work is hard, and you need to be in the right mindset to challenge these situations. Otherwise, it could cause further emotional trauma.

Letting go of shame and forgiving myself for staying quiet in those moments was the first step. Protecting my own mental health was important and, in those early circumstances, I did not have the tools to confront these difficult issues.

Now, after much work, I take one conversation at the time. If I feel like the person is open to feedback and self-examination,

I embark on these hard topics. My favorite way to react to discriminatory statements is with a simple response:

"Tell me more about that..."

"Tell me why you feel that way..."

If you try this, you will find that when people have to explain themselves or the statements they just made *and* they understand that you are not agreeing with them, they start to pause and self-reflect a little bit more. They start to hear what they themselves are saying a little bit more. They examine a little bit more. At that point, a fruitful discussion can start.

Being Someone You Are Not Is Emotionally Exhausting

At the beginning of this chapter, I explained that going along with the mainstream can seem easy.

Stay quiet.

Keep everyone comfortable.

Go along with the crowd.

But, as I have said before, being someone you are not or staying quiet when those around you are disapproving of your identity will eventually take its toll. For the individual, altering yourself to blend in with the mainstream eventually leads to alienation and disconnection. If you are not truly sharing who you are authentically, you become detached from your peers. So instead of spending energy on brainstorming new, innovative ideas or how to approach the next problem at work, you spend it on worries about what you need to hide to fit in with your co-workers.

The toll of hiding is also not limited to ordinary folks like you and me. It can happen to anyone, including a princess. In her famous interview with Oprah Winfrey, Meghan Markle, Duchess of Sussex and wife of Prince Harry, who is the younger son of Prince Charles and Lady Diana Spencer and sixth in the line of succession to the British throne, revealed the costs of hiding her true self from the public eye. She is a woman of mixed race entering a centuries-long institution, and she found that the royal family was not ready to welcome her with open arms. She walked into this situation with the intent of serving and fulfilling her responsibilities as a princess but quickly learned that she had to do it according to the rules they had put in place. Even as the tabloids were destroying who she was, she was unable to speak up and defend herself. She also faced racism from inside her own family, who made comments about the color of her new baby's skin. This led to a decline in Meghan Markle's mental health as she struggled to make sense of it all. When she asked for support from the royal family, she was denied it, because they felt it was shameful to acknowledge that a member of the royal family was suffering from a mental health condition. So, she was forced to live a life of silence until she could do it no longer. This, she said, eventually led to the point where she did not want to live anymore. Thankfully, she had the courage to tell her husband about her suicidal thoughts and, with that revelation, started on the road to healing.

During the interview, Prince Harry stated, "I was trapped, and I didn't even know it."

I was trapped, and I didn't even know it. I think that adequately describes what it feels like when you are hiding a part of your identity from the world. It usually starts out with little justifications on why you can handle it and why it makes sense not to rock the boat.

"It's better if I don't say anything."

"I'm just going to ignore those comments and not let it affect me."

"I'll just keep [insert anything] a secret. I don't want to embarrass my family."

"I can handle all this. I'm tough."

One after another, we make up excuses to protect ourselves. But instead, these excuses begin chipping away at our whole existence. And with each denial, we get deeper and deeper into it a hole, with no ladder and no way to get out. That is when you have to make a choice. You can stay in that hole and deny yourself a life that makes you happy, or you can have the courage and vulnerability to start to slowly climb out of it.

MANAGER STRATEGIES

Many of your employees are likely hiding a part of themselves because of their fear of not belonging. Creating a culture of belonging begins with creating a safe space for your employees to show up as their authentic selves. As a manager, here are some things you can do to learn more about your employees so that they don't have to stay in hiding.

Proactively commemorate different cultural or religious celebrations. Learn about what different ethnicities, cultures, identities or religions may be celebrating at any given time during the year and be curious about it. Don't just observe Christmas and Easter.

Conduct regular check-ins with your employees. Regularly ask your employees how they are feeling—really feeling—particularly during times of change, transition or social unrest. For example, if your employee is about to go out on parental leave, check in on them and see how it's going without waiting for them to come to you when they need to adjust their hours to accommodate new childcare responsibilities. Be proactive and ask them what you can do to support them during this major life transition.

Don't ignore what's happening in the outside world. If there are events of violence in the news based on race, ethnicity, religion, sexual orientation or gender identity, for example, check in on your employees who are part of that identity. They may be suffering silently and in need of some space to process the event. Don't expect them to show up at a meeting with a smile on their face, excited to give you their weekly report (although they likely will). Instead, proactively ask whether they may need some extra time on any assignments or some time off to process the events of the day. This one small gesture will make your employee feel seen and connected to your organization.

4

You Are Enough

I
T WAS late 2016 and I was sitting in my therapist's office. She held her sessions out of her home, giving our time a much more comfortable feel. It was like I was meeting a best friend for coffee and a chat. I would take the thirty-minute drive up the long windy roads in the mountains of Santa Cruz to get to my sessions, always losing reception during the last five minutes of the drive, which gave me some time to think. It was always worth the commute to go talk with Deb. I don't take that for granted anymore.

For most of my life, I never considered going to a therapist, let alone admit publicly that I went to one. The stigma around "needing" a therapist was far too large for me. Family members would often say that we don't need to work out our problems with a therapist or in public. Our problems are private and meant to stay within the family. I believed that I was somehow weak if I couldn't get through my stuff on my own.

You are enough, Deb said to me one day during one of our sessions.

I don't remember exactly what I had just told her. I was probably rambling about one of the millions of things I was juggling and how I felt like I was failing at all of them.

"Getting all these things done perfectly or making everyone around you happy does not define your worth. You are worthy for simply being you. *You are enough*," Deb explained.

As someone who had been hustling all her life trying to prove to everyone around me that I was enough, that I belonged, it hadn't dawned on me that the only person I needed to convince was myself. All my life I had searched for someone other than myself to validate my worth. Things that were important to me were:

- Gold stars from my teachers

- Approval from my family

- Accolades and promotions at work

- Invitations from friends or colleagues to join them at the latest event

I wanted others to tell me I was enough, was worthy of their approval or acceptance, yet I never looked within to realize that I was enough simply for being born.

You are enough.

Three simple words that can change the way you look at yourself.

Three simple words that can change how you show up in the world.

Three simple words that give you permission to make mistakes and still be okay.

You are enough.

As much as I wanted to, I did not believe those three words for a very long time.

For Latinas in the workforce this is particularly difficult. The Latino culture and values are different from the traditional corporate culture. According to Network of Executive Women,

53 percent of Latinas say that executive presence at their company conforms to traditionally white male standards. This means that the majority of Latinas feel as though they can't be themselves at work and feel valued at the same time. For example, we were raised to respect our elders and authority figures, which in a traditional corporate culture hinders our ability to self-promote or push boundaries at work. We also tend to use facial expressions, language and hand gestures to communicate our thoughts, which may be perceived as too loud or distracting in a traditional workplace. I've had people tell me to "tone it down" or that I have a "big personality." You hear these comments and quickly learn to adapt to the environment around you, and then, in a flash, your authentic self begins to disappear. You start minimizing the personality traits that make you uniquely you. It is no surprise that after a while you begin to believe that you are not enough.

You Are More Interesting Than You Realize

As you know by now, I kept my Latina identity hidden in an effort to protect myself. It never occurred to me that some people would actually be *interested* in that part of me, that some people would think that part of me was rich and valuable.

But one day, when I was sitting in Deb's office, I started to realize that my ethnicity is an interesting part of who I am. That it is, in fact, something special.

"Tell me about where you are from and your parents," Deb said.

"My mom is from El Salvador and my dad is from Ecuador and they met in Los Angeles."

Her eyes lit up and her arms flung high in the air with excitement, "Fantastic! That is absolutely beautiful. I want to hear more about them!"

I sat stunned in my chair. Deb was so thrilled to hear that my family was from Latin America. She wanted to learn more about my parents' love story and how they each got to the United States, their first jobs, and on and on. All of it. She was so intrigued. As I told her about my family and their immigration story, she asked whether I had shared any of this part of me at work.

"No," I quickly blurted out. "I don't talk about any of it at work. I don't want anyone to know where I am from."

Her entire body sunk in her chair. She stared at me from behind her glasses with a dejected look on her face.

"I am so sad to hear that," Deb said. "This is such a beautiful part of who you are."

I was speechless. In that moment I realized I had never thought of my ethnicity as something beautiful. I had always thought of it as something that could harm me. I was actually surprised to hear that being Latina was something Deb thought was interesting, and that others would love to hear about as well. From overt racist comments to subtle slights, society had been telling me that the world thought differently. I believed that I would be treated as inferior if co-workers and friends knew I was Latina. I had created so much fear around this belief that it led me to leave that part out of my story. It left a gaping hole.

As Deb and I talked, she encouraged me to think about what it might feel like to share this part of my identity at the workplace. She asked me to think about how me showing up as my authentic self might give others the freedom to do the same thing. She reminded me of how few Latinas there are in leadership, and that *I* could be the Latina leader I had so desperately wanted to see when I was a young person starting out. I could be a role model and perhaps make it easier for other people to bring their whole selves to work. That is when I decided to open up about my heritage. But it took some time.

The Slow Reveal

Fully embracing and subsequently sharing my Latina identity has not been easy. I was nervous about being rejected. That all changed after that life-changing session with Deb. In that moment, I realized I could no longer downplay or cover my heritage. That not only was my ethnic background interesting and beautiful, I also had a responsibility to all other Latinas to display it proudly on their behalf.

Slowly, I started sharing parts of my background. I began to talk about my parents and my family in El Salvador and Ecuador. In the beginning, it was little revelations to close friends about summer trips in Ecuador or my grandmother from El Salvador. In those first steps, I would sit and brace myself for their reaction.

Will it be positive or negative?

Will they think this is interesting and want to learn more or will I see a wall come up?

Will they start treating me differently?

Each time I shared a part of myself, I would wait in fear of the negative repercussions. If the worst happened, I would retreat back into my cave. If they seemed interested and curious about my background, then I would slowly reveal a little bit more. It was a song and dance each time. Once I felt safe enough with friends, I began to venture into harder spaces, like talking to co-workers or my manager.

The next step was to have the outer me match the inner me.

I started with what most people might not think twice about, but to me felt like outing myself: I decided to update my LinkedIn profile. To that point, if anyone went to look me up, they would likely think I was white. I had listed my college degrees without reference to my ethnic affinity organizations; my elite corporate jobs were listed one after another; a photo of me was posted with a conventional black suit and straight hair; my name simply read: "Tricia Timm."

This was the platform where all those whose approval I so desperately sought resided. It was the place that felt the riskiest. So, with tremendous trepidation, I started adding and changing a few words on my profile to reveal my Latina identity.

The first thing I did was to add "Spanish" as one of the languages I spoke. Many people speak Spanish who are not Latino so that wasn't too much of a stretch, but it was a start.

Next, I added my maiden name, Montalvo. I was particularly pleased about this change as it would certainly identify me as non-white. Next, I included all the Latino organizations I've been a part of over the years, such as La Raza and the Hispanic National Bar Association. I knew that this would certainly label me as a Latina for anyone who read my full bio.

The real test came when *Hispanic Executive* magazine decided to run a story about me. I was excited to do the article, but then it hit me. *If I do this article and it is published, then the whole world will know I am Latina.* How was this going to change things for me? Would I be perceived as an "activist"? Would people assume that my accomplishments were not deserved because of affirmative action or some other corporate diversity mandate? My mind raced with so many what-if scenarios:

What if the people I respect no longer respect me?

What if the executives, board members and recruiters I have nurtured relationships with now see me negatively?

What if folks start seeing me as someone who might cause problems in the workplace?

As these scenarios circled through my mind, one recurring thought that Deb had seeded also showed up:

What if, by sharing my story, I inspire other Latinas who struggle to feel like they belong?

This thought stayed in the back of mind. As I reflected back on my career, I remembered how difficult it was to never be able to see anyone who looked like me in the room. By staying quiet and hidden, I had not only robbed myself of the joy of openly sharing the details of my life with others, I had, more importantly, robbed millions of other Latinas of the chance to see what they could accomplish or become. Instead of pulling others up, I had sat at the table alone. I decided in that moment that, instead of being the "only," I wanted to be the "first." I wanted to be the first of many more to come after me. I realized that this begins with me showing up authentically and working to normalize my culture and ethnicity so that others can do the same.

So, I did the *Hispanic Executive* article. In that piece I proudly talked about my family and where I came from. The cat was out of the proverbial bag.

When the article was published, I received accolades from co-workers. All of my fears about people treating me as "less than" in the workplace did not come true. In fact, what happened next was not what I expected. As the *Hispanic Executive* feature circulated on social media, other Latinas who were either lawyers or in tech positions started sending me messages to thank me for telling my story. One young Latina told me she had never met anyone else in her career whose mom was from El Salvador, and that it was so nice to finally meet someone who has a parent from the same country. Another Latina told me how emotional she got when she read about another lawyer in tech with an Ecuadorian background. What I didn't realize was that not only is my story interesting to people because it is unique and different, those with similar backgrounds are also grateful to see someone like them who has achieved success. It means it is possible for them, too.

When I first started embracing my Latina identity, I was scared of what past co-workers might think about me. While I did imagine that most of them would simply say something like, "Huh, I didn't know she was Latina," and then move on with their day, I still feared that I would be looked upon differently. That I would not be good enough. Eventually I let that fear go, but it took some time. As I continued to get more involved with affinity organizations and saw what my visibility was doing to uplift others, I knew I had done the right thing. Now, as I look at my LinkedIn profile and see all the changes I made to it, I smile. It has been a long journey, but I am finally proud of where I came from. Have I completely let go of all my fears and fully uncovered my true self? Not really. I still go by Tricia instead of Patricia. I still have my married name attached to my identity. I even struggled with the decision of what name to put on the front cover of this book. I love the name Patricia, but I only use it with my family members in Ecuador or when I introduce myself to someone who speaks Spanish. I've always been called Tricia at work and with friends, so that is what feels authentic to me right now. That may change over time, or it may not. I don't know. I've been Tricia Timm for so long that it is also a part of my identity. Can you have dual identities? I'm not sure.

Self-acceptance is a journey and, like you, I am still on that journey. While I've made a ton of progress, I know there is more to learn and more ways to grow. I know that I must be patient with myself and trust the process.

You Are More Interesting *to Others* Than You Realize

It's amazing how you can convince yourself that you are not enough. That you don't deserve to be in the room. That your native language is not as good as the English language. That your family is not as impressive as "that" family. That your choices in clothes and cuisine are wrong. The list can go on and on. But there is a flip side to this equation. What if, instead of thinking that you are not enough, you think that you *are* enough. That all the little things that make you different are not in fact bad things, but *good* things. That they make you more interesting. That you bring something of value to the world.

In September 2021 I was invited by a company to speak to their Latino employee resource group during National Hispanic Heritage Month. I agreed, and since we were still under COVID-19 protocols, we did the presentation via video. I decided I would simply recycle the same presentation I had done at Looker years earlier. So, I joined the call and started telling my story. But, unlike last time (when I didn't receive feedback until after the presentation was over), this time I was receiving real-time feedback in the video chat.

Here are a few of the comments I read that day as I gave my presentation:

I feel this name change in my bones.

I felt the same way at my very white private university. The custodial staff became like my family away from home. I thought I was the only one.

When you're around people of your similar identity there's comfort in that—comunidad is so important!

For some reason, I continued to be surprised by how interested people were in my story. I am the child of two immigrant parents, I went to school, got good grades and worked hard. Head down. That's it. That's how I view my life. Nothing out of the ordinary.

I periodically glanced at the video screen as I spoke, at all the eyes staring right back at me in careful attention. When I told certain parts of my story, particularly the vulnerable pieces, heads nodded in agreement. Some people had tears streaming down their faces. Following the presentation, one Latina told me what an impact my story had on her and how inspiring it was for her to see me speak. It is these small moments that remind me that people are more interested in me than I realize.

The same is true for you and your personal story. I have no doubt that there is richness in your truth that someone could benefit from hearing. Think about the good that could come from you sharing it. What if, instead of only focusing on the times when people look down on your differences, you leaned into the times when people appreciate those differences?

So, what is holding us back from telling our stories?

SELF-REFLECTION MOMENT

- Do you find the personal stories and histories of others interesting?

- When people share details about their favorite foods, or their family history, or their relationship with their grandparents, do you judge them? You probably don't—so why not offer the benefit of the doubt to the people who are listening to you?

How to Manage Negative Self-Talk

We all can say to ourselves three simple words: "You are enough." The hard part is not in saying it, it is in actually believing it. Really believing it. Not just repeating the words. The first step toward believing that you are enough is examining why you didn't think you were enough in the first place. This can stem from many different reasons, but for me it started with all the messages I had received growing up. I had internalized the belief that I had to be better than everyone around me in order to belong. I had to be perfect.

So, unwittingly, I became a perfectionist. Seems like a good thing, right? In some cases, it was. It enabled me to achieve great success in my life. Award winner in school. Promotions at work. The ultimate "gold stars" in about almost everything I did. While, to some, perfectionism may seem like a small problem, it has an ominous side that few talk about. Many who suffer from perfectionism don't realize it. I didn't realize it until my mid-forties. Perfectionism is a quiet little voice inside you that is always telling you that you are not enough.

My writing doesn't make sense.

My presentation is too long.

This email has a typo in it.

I don't have enough experience.

The chatter is constant. Everything you do comes with an inner commentary telling you it is not quite good enough. You keep trying to make yourself better or more able to quiet the disappointed voices in your head. Often these voices are so subtle you don't notice them. They are just these inner feelings that keep telling you to work harder, to make whatever you are doing just a little bit better.

I'm all for high achievement. Striving for excellence is good. But perfectionism is more than that. It is the constant feeling that whatever you are doing is not good enough. The problem with perfectionism is that you can never internalize your accomplishments. You can never really appreciate your successes because you only accept things that are done perfectly as worthy of your appreciation. Ironically, perfectionism is fueled by those moments when someone praises you for your flawless work. That "high" you get when you hear the words "This is perfect!"

To a perfectionist, these words are irreplaceable. They fill your body with an overwhelming sense of joy and calmness. For a very brief moment, you feel completely worthy. Fully complete. *Enough.*

Until . . . the next project, email, or presentation comes along. And the vicious cycle of negative self-talk starts all over again. The mistakes. The doubts. The worries. All the chatter begins to fill your brain again. It is exhausting and never-ending.

For so many years, I wanted to ignore it, stuff it down or get angry about this part of me. I wanted to be more like my husband, who never seemed to be fazed by his mistakes. When he messed up, he would shrug it off, say, "My bad!" and move on. He would not spend days spinning about it.

Why couldn't I just brush things off without a worry like my husband? Why were mistakes so easy for him to make and then get over? Why couldn't I forgive myself for making a mistake? That was all I wanted. I wanted the freedom of not having to be perfect all the time.

Unfortunately, many of us, particularly people of color, suffer from this vicious cycle.

So, how do you end it?

Author Ethan Kross provided several helpful tools on an episode of the podcast *The Happiness Lab* with Dr. Laurie Santos. Kross suggests there is no evidence that we can stop negative thoughts from entering our minds, but once activated, instead of trying to ignore them, we can *control* what we do with them. When negative chatter enters our mind, we have a choice. We can either narrowly zoom in and amplify it, which leads us down the rabbit hole of worries, insecurities and fears, or we can choose to zoom out and minimize it, transform it or replace it with other thoughts. Here are a few strategies that Kross suggests for combating negative self-talk:

Use "distanced self-talk." This is when we try to coach ourselves through a problem using our own name or the second person pronoun "you." Instead of saying, "What should I do?" you can say, "What would you do, Tricia?" We are much better at giving advice to others than giving advice to ourselves. By changing the language in which we talk to ourselves, we put ourselves in advisory mode, which makes it much easier for us to work through our problems.

Use mental time travel. We can distance ourselves from the experience with time. Ask yourself: "How am I going to feel about this issue tomorrow, next week, next year, in ten years?" This technique reminds us that no matter how awful the experience might feel in the moment, eventually it will get better. It puts that painful experience into perspective.

Activate an alter ego. How would someone we admire handle the situation? For me, I often think about how my husband Derek would react, since he doesn't tend to dwell on things. However, Kross warns us to be sure to pick the right alter ego. You want to hear the voice of the supportive coach and not the critical parent, for example.

Normalize your experience. When we are stuck in negative dialogues, we might feel like we are the only one experiencing it. Realizing that you are not alone is very useful. For example, in writing this book I learned that it is common for first-time authors to have inner critics. We think things such as, "Who would want to read this book anyways?" or "There are millions of books like this already out there, what makes mine unique?" When such negative thoughts popped up, it was comforting to know that others had gone through this same experience and it was normal.

For perfectionists, negative chatter pops up frequently. If you often beat yourself up for "doing it wrong" or making a mistake or not being the best at something, I am here to tell you that it is okay to love and accept that perfectionist part of you. That's right, I said, *love* that part of you. That part of you is here to make you better. It is here to protect you from a world that has put up a lot of obstacles in front of your success. Instead of trying to change that part of yourself, what if you simply paused for a moment and appreciated this part of you that has made you so successful in life? It has served a wonderful purpose. Without it, you may not have achieved as much as you have.

NEXT SMALL THING
The next time negative self-talk starts to show up in your mind, test out one of the four strategies offered by Ethan Kross on that podcast. Try a different strategy every time it happens. Which feels most natural? Which is most effective?

The Wave Theory

Learning how to notice negative self-talk when it shows up was an important first step toward self-acceptance for me. The second was realizing that life goes in periods of expansion and contraction and that both are essential. This was best described to me in terms of examining how waves work.

Have you ever looked at the waves of an ocean? According to the National Ocean Service, "waves are created by energy passing through water, causing it to move in a circular motion." If you sit and look at waves, you will see a series of expansions and contractions, one after another. Some waves are big and come crashing down onto the shore with the weight of the ocean behind them and others come up onto the sand gently, one following the other.

Which wave are you in your life right now?

This is the question Deb posed to me during one of my visits with her. She explained that our lives are a series of waves. We have periods of expansion and periods of contraction. In periods of expansion, everything is going well. This is when you are in your flow. It is during this time that people start new things, transition into a career change, foster new relationships or go on new adventures. Expansion is an exciting time, and we continue growing, expanding and intensifying during this phase, until it is too much. At some point along this expanding wave, there likely comes a moment when suddenly you are out of your flow. Decisions get harder. Relationships are strained. Your job may have become unfulfilling. Some notice it, others do not. If you do notice it, that is when there is a decision to make. Do you artificially push harder to stay on that wave and risk coming crashing down, or do you intentionally decide that it is time to slow down and enter the contraction phase?

In periods of contraction, everything is at rest. The wave is getting ready to expand again but it pauses, regroups and slowly comes over the warm sand to rest before starting all over again. During periods of contraction, your mind and body get to rest. Many high achievers like to pass over this period of contraction. We may have been told by cultural norms that resting is lazy. That not going for that additional project or role is not being ambitious enough. That to be successful you need to be productive. Whatever the story we have in our heads, something is holding us back from enjoying the period of contraction. What I learned, however, is that to have a successful period of expansion, one must first go through a period of contraction. In fact, if you do not have this period of contraction, your wave will just come crashing down.

The goal in life is not to have big, expansive waves followed by big crashes, but instead to have a continuous set of small waves, which gently come and go through life. If you can manage that, you can have great periods of expansion where big and wonderful things will happen without that huge crash that can result in burnout, exhaustion, loss of friends or even the loss of a marriage. If you pay attention to many of the different personal stories that appear throughout this book, you will notice how everyone seems to go through a period of contraction prior to a period of expansion.

When Your Authentic Self Does Not Get You What You Want

There will be times when you might go out on a limb and reveal something vulnerable about yourself, and you will fall flat. An email or a phone call will go unanswered, you won't get the promotion or position you wanted, or you will say something to a room and receive only blank stares. In these moments, you realize that your authentic self is not welcomed.

Not all of us have the financial or emotional security to just forge ahead despite all of the potentially unpleasant consequences of showing up authentically. Early in my career, when I was the sole breadwinner for my family, I did not feel like I had the freedom to speak up and challenge the inequities at my then-current job. At the time, I also did not have the support system at work or in my personal life to back me up when I felt defeated. For those who are currently in this situation, give yourself permission to do what you have to do to protect yourself and your family. We are not all at the same place in life. Sometimes we need to recognize where we are at and give ourselves some grace.

For those ready for a change, I hope this book is the beginning of your journey to self-acceptance. Once you believe that you are enough, you will have more strength and courage to challenge those times that your authentic self is not valued. For me, once I fully embraced my true self, I could no longer show up in any other way. Hiding and staying quiet was no longer a choice.

MANAGER STRATEGIES

There is power in storytelling. By hearing and sharing each other's stories, we begin to create connection and empathy. What can you do to encourage storytelling at work?

Create a "Storytelling Hour" at your company. This could be held monthly, quarterly or during certain cultural awareness events. It is especially important to encourage executives or other senior leaders to participate and tell their stories. Everyone has had to overcome something hard in their lives, and simply hearing that others have faced adversity and that you are not alone can make all the difference. The more vulnerable the leader, the stronger the culture will be.

Establish Employee Resource Groups (ERGs). Create a safe place for employees to support each other through ERGs and similar communities. Ensure that the ERGs you create have sufficient budget to plan activities and gather. ERG-sponsored events are a great place for employees to share their stories.

Enlist executive sponsorship for ERGs. Consider having an executive who does *not* identify with a particular group sponsor that ERG. For example, at one company, the male CEO became the executive sponsor for the Mom's ERG, and got to hear first-hand from working mothers about the struggles of juggling work and family life. This gave him more insight and empathy when it came time for the annual review of health benefits and parental leave policies. This approach gives executives an opportunity to learn about an identity they were not previously familiar with—something that can lead to meaningful change within an organization.

Ensure that the executive team is actively involved in your DEI initiatives. Many companies feel like all they have to do is hire a head of diversity and then their DEI problem is solved. Nothing is further from the truth. As Dr. Gena Cox tells us in her book *Leading Inclusion*, it is essential that the members of your executive team, especially the CEO, are actively involved in all aspects of the program in order for it to be successful. Employees are looking for executive teams who are genuinely examining their workplace, doing the work and making positive changes—not just window dressing.

5

Belonging Begins
with Self-Acceptance

F OR ALEXANDRA NAVARRO, who you first met in Chapter 2,
the road to self-acceptance has been a slow journey of
self-discovery. Back in Colombia, Alexandra was important
and someone with opportunities. She was a sought-after speaker
and was even featured on television, but when she arrived in the
United States, she was nobody. In her words, "less than nobody."
She knew she had so many talents to share with the world but
could not find a way to use them effectively. Two versions of
Alexandra soon developed as she traveled back and forth from
Colombia. She didn't know who she was and where she belonged.
She no longer felt like she belonged in Colombia and she knew
that she did not fit in the U.S. The Geo Metro incident, in which her
co-workers mocked her car, confirmed that for her. She felt lost.

Not surprisingly, during this time Alexandra also grew disconnected from her husband and children. In fact, most of the
time she only wanted to be with her mom and dad. She didn't
have much money and was emotionally drained. She felt hope-
less and like she had hit rock bottom.

Realizing that something needed to change, Alexandra asked her husband if she could take some time away from the family to rediscover herself. So, for the next year, she traveled, met the Pope and the Dalai Lama and went inward to try to understand her emotions and purpose. Alexandra was experiencing her contraction phase. She wanted to find the resources she needed to be able to respond with compassion when she was mistreated. It was during this self-discovery process that she identified her core values of family, faith and authenticity. These three values are now her guiding light in any situation.

Alexandra returned to her family and started a new life by approaching situations from a place of compassion rather than judgment. She also realized that life was a series of Geo Metro moments and our job is to learn how to respond to them. With each moment, you learn and grow to become a better version of you. Each time, you are showing up more authentically. Now, let's look at the steps you can take to start letting go of your fears and all the expectations of those around you and begin living the life you deserve.

Quitting Is Not Always the Answer

For all of us who have tried to be someone we are not, Alexandra's story is very familiar. For me, I was constantly trying to say the right things, look a certain way and play the proper roles. After a while it became exhausting. What I didn't realize was that I didn't need to do all that. That the only thing I needed to be was myself, and that self did not have to be perfect and did not have to fit nicely into anyone's preconceived box. That learning did not come easily or quickly. I thought that quitting would be the answer.

After fifteen years as a corporate lawyer, I was exhausted from trying to belong. I never felt like I could live up to the idolized standard of what a corporate lawyer should be, so I felt inadequate. When I turned forty-four, I decided to leave my cushy general counsel job and began thinking about what to do next.

At first, I thought I would switch careers altogether. I'm not sure if this is what they call a mid-life crisis, but out of nowhere I started questioning my whole life. I began exploring different occupations, such as becoming a legal recruiter or head of DEI, which at the time was a new type of role. I ultimately chose to stick with the lawyer thing but decided to start my own legal consulting business. I thought that running my own business under my own terms would free me from having to conform to the expectations of others. I assumed that by working alone I would not have to endure the daily pretending that I had become so accustomed to in the traditional corporate setting. So, I leased a small office for myself and called it the "She-Shed," got a new puppy for some companionship and started my own company. Alone.

At first, my new business was everything I had dreamed of. The flexibility to spend more time with my family, a place where I could show up in my T-shirt and jeans and not be judged, and exciting clients and assignments to maintain my legal skills. In just one short year, I grew the company to over a million dollars in annual revenue, a milestone that is reached by less than 2 percent of all women entrepreneurs. By all external factors, my new company was a great success. Many of my former colleagues were envious of how quickly I was able to launch a thriving business. Yet, I continued to feel unfulfilled.

I was sitting alone in my small office. As I looked around, I noticed that, while I was proudly showing up to work every day in this new workspace that I had created, nobody was there. I was alone. Rather than showing up in the world as my authentic self, I was instead hiding my authentic self from the world.

I had sequestered myself into a small office with my dog. I had hoped that, in this office by myself, I would be safe from daily microaggressions. Here, I would not have to wake up every day and put on a facade to try to belong in an environment I did not feel welcomed in. I had convinced myself that, if I were alone, I would find peace.

But that was not the case. In fact, the opposite happened. Instead of feeling happy, I felt lonely. No one to chitchat with about my kids. No social events where I could laugh with my co-workers. No employees to mentor. I had not realized how important things like community and purpose had been in my career and in my life. In an effort to protect myself from the daily grind of uncomfortable comments or situations, I had isolated myself from the world.

Brené Brown's words echoed in my ears as I tried to figure out why I was unhappy with the situation I had created.

True belonging doesn't require us to change who we are; it requires us to be who we are.

I just needed to be who I was, all the time—the confident Latina girl who enjoyed wearing a T-shirt and jeans and had a loud laugh. It was that simple. I didn't have to wear suits and dresses that screamed I was a corporate lawyer. I didn't have to remain silent when my ideas were brushed off. I didn't have to pretend that raising kids while working full-time was a walk in the park. I could stop pretending, take off the mask and just be me.

With this newfound revelation, I thought the next step would be easy. I believed that I could simply flip a switch. Unfortunately, it was *not* that easy. The problem was that the strong, confident Latina girl in me had left me many years before. She was hiding behind so much armor that she wasn't sure she could make herself vulnerable again. The idea of revealing my true self to the outside world felt too risky.

SELF-REFLECTION MOMENT

- Take a moment to think about the real you. Have you had a Geo Metro moment?

- What masks would you remove and what parts of your identity would you reveal if you had nothing to lose?

- Who in your life supports you in removing your mask and being yourself?

- Who in your life is preventing you from removing your mask?

Where Did That Confident Little Latina Girl Go?

When I was ten years old, I was fearless. I loved sports and competing. I enjoyed school and was always at the top of my class. I also liked having fun. At recess you could find me either playing volleyball with my friends or running around playing tag with the boys. I look back at this time fondly. I was carefree and invincible—as carefree as I could be in a Catholic school. I didn't know then, but soon that fearless, carefree little Latina girl would be told she was too much and not enough all at the same time.

I went to school in a predominantly white suburban neighborhood. I was only one of a handful of Black or brown kids at my school. We lived in Southern California so there was a high percentage of Latinos living in the area and many were working as gardeners, farmers or housekeepers. I often heard classmates refer to Latinos using slurs and offensive names, and instinctually knew that I needed to distance myself from being Latino if I were to be accepted in this environment.

The little things that were said to me along the way also led me to believe that being Latino was somehow "lesser than" being white. My mother loved keeping our house meticulous, so on the weekends she would throw on her favorite flowered nightgown and slippers and spend most of her time cleaning and preparing our meals for the week. When new friends came into the house, they often mistook my mother for the house-keeper. They would tell me how nice "my maid" was. My heart sank every time. My mother was an accomplished banker—in fact, she was the manager at the local bank—but my classmates only saw her as the maid. I was embarrassed for us both. These comments may have been innocent, but the pain of how I felt in those moments stuck with me.

Back at school, I was considered "too much." I had a loud laugh and loved to talk with friends. I was a straight-A student, except for conduct. Yes, we had a conduct grade and it was always a C for me. I argued with my parents that it wasn't that I was talking more, it was just that my voice and laugh was louder than the other kids and so the teachers noticed it more. I'm still sticking to that story! The sisters also didn't understand why I liked running around with the boys. It was not a very ladylike thing to do, they would tell me. I was just playing tag.

While I was considered "too much" at school, I was at the same time not good enough. I learned that lesson quickly when I wanted to become an altar server. Being part of a parochial school meant that we were required to attend Mass. If you have never been to a Catholic Mass, you need to know that they are very ritualistic. Readings, prayers, hymns, gestures and the sacrament of the Holy Communion. We all rise up and down simultaneously, sitting and kneeling at just the right moment in the prayer. We repeat the same prayers during each Mass, with only the readings and the gospel changing from Mass to Mass. As a kid, these prayers got seared into my brain so well that I could repeat them without realizing what I was saying. Not surprisingly, as a young person, this event got pretty boring after a while.

Something that stood out about those Catholic Masses, though, were the altar boys who assisted the priests. They wore fancy robes and collars and participated during the ceremony. They got to walk down the aisle, carry the cross, light the candles and present the bread and wine to the priest. They were kept busy the whole time. This seemed so interesting to me and a way to make Mass more fun.

One day I decided that I wanted to become an altar boy. I wanted to dress up in the robes and help with the Mass.

"Sister Mary, can I please sign up to be an altar boy for the next Mass?"

"Patricia, I'm sorry, but you can't sign up. You must be a boy to sign up."

"Why do you have to be a boy?"

I was genuinely puzzled. I guess I knew they were called "altar boys" but I really didn't stop to think what that meant. I couldn't think of a reason why this role would be exclusively for boys. The crosses were not too heavy to carry (which, I know, shouldn't be a reason by itself anyway), and I could not think of any other justification for this absurd limitation.

"It's just the way it is," Sister Mary said. "There are only altar boys. No altar girls."

I stared at her, trying to make sense of what she had just told me. *I couldn't do something just because I was a girl.* Immediately, I knew what I had to do.

"We need to change that rule then, Sister Mary. That doesn't make any sense." I was starting to get mad now. "Who do I need to talk to? I'll go see the principal about it. I'm not scared to do that."

Sister Mary looked at me with a puzzled face. I don't think she quite knew how to respond to me or handle this question.

"Well, it's not up to the principal. You will need to talk with the Pope. Only the Vatican can change this rule."

Silence.

Thinking.

"Okay, then we need to call the Pope."

It seemed like the only thing we could do. I also knew that we *had* to do it.

Needless to say, they did not put me in touch with the Pope and I did not change the Vatican's rule that day. For the rest of my time in elementary school, I was not permitted to be an altar server. Nobody in the school administration agreed with me that this was a silly rule, and I found no support for my call to change it. This was the first time I learned about limitations because of my gender. No matter how hard I could try, the mere fact that I was female would prohibit me from doing something I wanted to do. So, for the rest of my school-age years, I sat in the pews during Mass, reciting my prayers and watching as a spectator while the boys roamed around the altar. It wasn't until 1994 that the Vatican approved girls serving at the altar during Roman Catholic Mass. That is one year after I graduated law school. It took that long. And women still cannot be Catholic priests today.

When people are perplexed to hear that I have imposter syndrome or can't believe that I still doubt myself, I have to explain to them the context in which I grew up. As I reflect back on my childhood, I realize that I started putting on armor as a young girl to protect myself. When you do this, eventually, without noticing, you are wearing a whole coat of metal.

I wish that self-acceptance was quick and easy. For some it might be, but for others, like me, it was not. It is not a quick fix because self-acceptance requires you to completely re-train how you think of yourself. Some of us may only have a little bit of armor, but some of us may have decades and decades of it, so thick that not even the fiercest of gladiators could pierce through it. That's the impenetrable defense system that I had created for myself. My armor was not going to come down easily. That confident, carefree little Latina girl had left many years ago.

Small Steps, Repeated Often

Letting go of perfectionism, learning to ignore negative self-talk and showing up in the world as your authentic self does not happen overnight. It is a series of small steps, repeated often, that will get you there. Knowing that the journey is a slow progression rather than a quick sprint keeps you grounded when you don't see immediate results. As a self-proclaimed Type-A person, I often had to remind myself—*small steps, repeated often*.

It was November 2016, and I was struggling to hold it all together. I was running my own business; taking care of my mother, who had fallen and injured her back; providing child care for my sister-in-law, who herself was battling postpartum depression; and, of course, attending to my own two daughters, who at the time were in grade school. I was trying to be all things, to all people, all of the time. I knew that I wasn't doing well emotionally, but I didn't know how to get better. So, I just pushed down my feelings and pressed on until my body finally told me that I could no longer do it. I started getting sick frequently; I lost focus, and couldn't get out of bed some days.

My friend Gina recommended I go see Doctor Rachel. Doctor Rachel is not like other doctors. She practices integrative medicine, which is a combination of Western and Eastern medicine. She is a board-certified medical doctor, so she can prescribe medications, but she spends time trying to figure out what is *causing* symptoms instead of just prescribing pills. So, for example, if I had a rash, she would dig in to see what was happening in my life that caused the rash rather than just giving me an ointment to treat it.

I recall every detail of that first appointment with Doctor Rachel. Her office was not like a typical doctor's office. She had an oversized comfy chair to sit in, a bookcase, a rug and a nice standing lamp in the corner. There were books on the shelves and art on the wall. I saw an exam table in the room, but it was off to the side like an afterthought and seemed like it was only used if necessary. Getting up on that table and putting your feet up in the stirrups is not why you go see Doctor Rachel. I remember feeling at home and comfortable in that room. I was curious to see what the appointment would be like.

She started by asking me to tell her what was going on. I sat there for what felt like hours as I told her my story, but it was likely only a few minutes.

"I haven't exercised in forever because my hip is injured. My body hurts."

"I can't remember the last time I slept through the night. I keep waking up with my mind racing."

"I am juggling so many things. Everyone expects me to save them. I feel completely overwhelmed."

The list went on and on. She sat and wrote her notes and listened with compassion.

At the end, she pulled out what seemed like a large medical pad and wrote me a "prescription":

☐ Do the work to reclaim *all* of you. See a therapist.

☐ Check out Brené Brown's TED talk on vulnerability.

☐ Take a beach volleyball class.

☐ For hip pain, see a physical therapist.

☐ Eat more fruits and vegetables. Carrot sticks, broccoli.

☐ For anxiety, try some herbal supplements.

Then she handed me a poem called *The Journey* by Mary Oliver. As she handed me these verses and my "prescription," tears ran down my face. In that moment, holding those two pieces of paper, I realized that my life was about to change. Without having the language to name it, I knew that she had just given me the prescription that would change my life.

This would not be easy work, but I had the playbook in my hand. I had the things I needed to transform myself. Everybody tells you to "get exercise and eat healthy" but the difference here was that we talked very specifically about what this would look like. I explained that I liked running but couldn't run because my hip hurt. She told me how to fix my hip and also offered some fun alternative choices to running, like playing beach volleyball. I told her that I was a picky eater so she started me off with just a few vegetables rather than trying to overhaul my entire diet. What I noticed in her notes and in every session to follow was one main theme. *Small steps repeated often.* I didn't have to change my whole lifestyle overnight. Just add carrot sticks one day, and repeat. Start with walking around the block during lunch. Repeat. Small steps, not big ones. And then, repeat.

To change a habit or a mindset, you need to practice. Trying to make a big wide sweeping change overnight rarely works. Expectations are too high and you ultimately fail, thus confirming to yourself that you are incapable of meeting that goal. But, if you start out with a very small, achievable goal, and then repeat it, that soon becomes a habit or a way of life. *Small steps, repeated often.*

I was surprised to learn that the theory of small steps, repeated often, is not a new one. I was listening to a podcast one day and the guest on this particular episode was the best-selling author James Clear. In his book *Atomic Habits*, he talks about the importance of small changes. He says that changes that seem unimportant at first will compound into remarkable results if you are willing to stick with them for years.

Clear uses the example of committing to doing daily push-ups. If you decide to do fifty push-ups every day, inevitably you will reach a day where you will be too tired to do fifty push-ups, so you decide not to do any. You skip push-ups that day. And probably for several days after that, until you are no longer doing any push-ups. Instead, if you had decided that you will only do *one* push-up every day, when that tired day comes, you know that you can do at least one push-up, so you do it. You won't see immediate results from the one push-up, but if you continue with doing it every single day, eventually you will see results. According to Clear, this is how you create healthy habits.

The hardest step is the first step. You will come up with a million reasons for why you can't do the thing. Nonetheless, when that feeling comes up, my advice to you is to move forward despite being scared. Once you get through a tough situation and realize that you can survive, your heart races a little bit less and your palms are a little less sweaty the next time.

Despite all my fears, I realized I had no choice but to follow Doctor Rachel's "prescription." Day after day, week after week, things slowly got better. The pain in my hip started to go away with physical therapy. I started to get more sleep, which helped with my anxiety. I signed up for that beach volleyball class and noticed I was smiling when I felt the sand between my toes and wind in my hair. I added carrots to dinner (admittedly, the broccoli took more time). I went to therapy and talked about the hard things. I cried a lot. I started doing the hard work.

One of the areas I needed to work on was my self-confidence. Through my therapy, I came to understand that my perfectionism was paralyzing me from trying new things because of my fear of failure. I decided that I needed to overcome that fear.

NEXT SMALL THING

Make a list of things in your life that are unhealthy habits. Are you not exercising enough? Not carving out enough time to spend with your friends? Not getting enough sleep? Whatever it is, just make a list of them.

Now, look at that list and pick just *one* thing to do. Not all, just one. Make a plan for how you will intentionally bring that one healthy thing back into your life, slowly. If you are not exercising enough, simply commit to walking for five minutes. Start small.

Once you have incorporated one new healthy habit, go back to your list and find the next thing. Just one, and repeat.

Practice Getting Comfortable with Rejection

Being rejected feels like the end of the world to some of us. In fact, if I could go through life without having to be rejected, sign me up! I always envy those people who can simply brush it off. They don't sit up at night and re-live the moment over and over again. They don't take things personally. They move on. I see this quality in entrepreneurs and salespeople. They have mastered the art of rejection. They had to. They would not be successful in their careers if they did not. For me, this has not been the case. I take rejection personally. I wonder what I did wrong. I wonder what is wrong with me. I wonder if there is something I could have done differently. The wonders can go and on and soon I am in a spiral of negative self-talk.

One tactic I've learned for getting over the fear and pain of rejection is to get desensitized to it. I learned this after listening to a TED talk called "What I Learned from 100 Days of

Rejection" by Jia Jiang. Jia set out on a journey to get over the fear of rejection by actively seeking it out for a hundred days in a row. Every day he would ask for something that he thought people would immediately reject.

The first thing he asked for was one hundred dollars from a stranger in a hotel lobby. Leading up to that moment, Jia said, his heart was racing, he was sweating, and it took him several tries to get up the courage to ask. When he finally asked for the hundred dollars, rather than being rejected, the person questioned what it was for. Instead of answering and possibly getting the money, Jia quickly ran away in fear. Because of that fear, he probably lost out on a hundred bucks.

Jia's "one hundred rejections" experiment spanned a number of hilarious requests, which included asking a fast-food restaurant for a "burger refill." Over and over again he was rejected, but, surprisingly, many times people actually helped him. With each try at asking for something bizarre, his fear of rejection lessened. Fewer knots in his belly. Less sweating. At the end of this research, Jia discovered that simply asking for what you want can open up more possibilities than you know. He realized that his fear of rejection was depriving him of new opportunities.

Practicing rejection helps us remove the importance we unconsciously place on the outcome of the answer. If we didn't care so much about the result, then taking the risk would not seem as scary. Jia suggests that, when you first start practicing with rejection, you should start out with little requests, where the rejection is of no consequence. Maybe ask the grocery store clerk for a free bag or ask a merchant for a discount. If they say no, what's the harm? You don't know them, and they don't know you, and you didn't expect it anyway. But imagine if they said yes.

Trust the Process

With Doctor Rachel's prescription in hand I continued to do the work, but, like every overachiever with a task ahead of her, I wanted to know exactly how long this transformation would take. Would it take a few days? Weeks? Months? I needed to know the timeline so I could map it out with my usual to-do lists and spreadsheets. I didn't have time for all this confusion, anxiety and sense of worthlessness. I was impatient and wanted results today.

The path to self-acceptance is not a quick one. I wish I could say that it will only take two weeks and you'll feel great again. Or that there is a magic pill that will make it all go away quickly. But, unfortunately, it does not work that way. Inevitably, you need to trust the process, however long it may take.

I remember when I first learned that there was no quick fix. It was either a Wednesday or a Thursday, and we had made plans to have our friends Neil and Jesse over for dinner. We hadn't seen them in a while, so a visit was overdue. I remember that moment because it was one of the hard ones. I didn't want to do anything that day. Even though I didn't have too much on my plate, every little thing felt completely overwhelming, including hosting a dinner party. All I wanted to do was curl up in my bed and watch TV for hours and hours. And that is exactly what I did for as long as I could. My husband knew that I did not have the capacity to put together a dinner, so I could hear him working away downstairs at preparing the house and the meal for our guests.

By the time Neil and Jesse arrived, I was able to muster the energy to get out of bed, get dressed and join the evening dinner. Jesse noticed my unusually low energy and asked how I was doing. This was not the first person who had asked me this question in the previous few weeks. I would always tell the same story. Things had been hard lately. I was tired and burned out, maybe a little depressed. The usual response I received was one of empathy and encouragement. I was told that things would get better soon and to hang in there. So, when Jesse asked me this familiar question, I expected the typical supportive response.

"How are you doing, Tricia?"

"Actually, not that great, Jesse. I don't know what's wrong with me. I just feel lost."

As I waited for the concerned look and the "you'll be okay, hang in there" response, something different happened. Jesse's eyes lit up and a huge smile came across her face.

"That is great news!" she shouted. "You are going through your transformation!"

She ran over and gave me a big hug like I had just announced I was getting married, having a baby or receiving a promotion. She was genuinely so excited for me and for what was to come. My discomfort was good news to her.

I was baffled. I had just told her how miserable and lost I was and she was happy for me. This didn't make sense. She explained that the struggle I was feeling was a good thing. That I was finally realizing that the life I had created was not supporting me anymore and that it was time for a change. She told me that this was where the real work begins. This was where I find my purpose in the world. This was all good news, she reassured me.

I decided to play along.

"Okay, fine. Let's assume you are correct," I said. "How long does this whole transformation thing take?"

I wasn't sure whether I believed this line of thinking but, for argument's sake, if it were true, I wanted to know exactly how long it would take for me to "transform" so that I could plan for it. Add it to my to-do list. I'm not sure how long you think a transformation might take, but in my mind, I was thinking one, maybe two weeks max. Based on how I felt in that moment, lonely and lost, I was not sure how much longer I would be able to endure, and I wanted reassurance that it was almost over. In my mind, I estimated that I could feel crappy for maybe a few more weeks but that would be it. I was ready to start feeling like my old self again.

"The whole thing takes maybe one to two years," she calmly told me.

"One to two *years!*" I blurted out. "Are you freakin' kidding me?"

The thought of feeling lost and without purpose for one to two years felt like an eternity.

"Trust the process," she told me. "I know it feels like a long time, but it is hard work and there is no shortcut. You have to simply go through it. Trust the process."

She was right. It took almost exactly two years from that day to transform into who I am today. Until I really felt like I could show up as my true self. Some days were good and some were bad, but slowly the good days outnumbered the bad days until one day I felt like a new person. It took work. Letting down one barrier at a time. Practicing being imperfect. Taking small risks. Then, repeat.

Being Vulnerable Takes Courage

It's funny how things appear when you are ready for them, and not one day before. It wasn't until I was feeling like a new person that the Looker opportunity appeared seemingly out of nowhere. I went into that job interview as the real me—the confident and casual Latina with a loud laugh. I truly believe that I got that job because I showed up as my authentic self. No more masks. No more pretense. I showed up exactly how I felt most comfortable... and the CEO seemed to actually appreciate it! In that state of being, I was able to continue the journey.

About three months after I started my new job at Looker, I decided to approach our CEO about building a DEI program. I was prepared for the "no." I had practiced rejection over and over by that point and knew that, if the answer was no, it would be okay. It would not mean I was less worthy for asking.

I remember walking into his office that day. I was only a few months into the job, and we were still getting to know one another. He was sitting back in his chair, ready for our weekly one-to-one. I went through our normal agenda items, and then he asked if there was anything else.

"Actually, yes," I said, as fear began to rise in my body.

"Sure, what's up?"

I told him that I wanted to help the company form a DEI program. I told him my story and gave him my reasons. Until that day, I had never told any of my managers where my parents were from. I had told no one that they had immigrated to this country from El Salvador or Ecuador. Nobody knew that Spanish was my first language. While I was scared to hear his response, I also felt free. No secrets. It felt so good to say out loud who I was and where I came from.

After I finished my story, he said: "Wow, that is such a great story. Yes, let's build a DEI program. In fact, I'd like you to lead it so that it gets the right visibility at the executive level."

This was not the reaction I had expected. I had spent so much time preparing for the rejection that I did not even know how to respond.

Finally, I said, "I would love to build it. Now, let's talk budget."

I walked out of that office with the biggest smile you have ever seen. Not only was I excited that we were going to start a DEI program, I was also so relieved that I had shared my personal story. No more hiding anymore. No more pretending. It wasn't until several years later that I made that LinkedIn post. I still had more growing to do myself. One of the best lessons I learned during those years at Looker was that we are always learning.

That was the beginning of an amazing DEI program at Looker. It only happened because I was able to shed my fears of rejection and was willing to show up as my authentic self with an idea. It took courage to be vulnerable.

However, it doesn't always work out that way. I don't want to pretend that it's all rainbows and unicorns. While this one day paid off, there were plenty of other days when it didn't work out. Sometimes you think about going to your boss's office, but you never make it there. Other days you make it to the office, but you don't ask the question. Then there are days when you muster the courage to ask, and you get rejected or ignored. Each of these moments are not failures. They are steps forward. Every time you try, it counts. What matters is continuing to try. Then, one day, one magical day, you will get the response you were hoping for.

The willingness to be vulnerable requires practice. It doesn't come out of nowhere. It's hard and requires a lot of work. It's like training for a marathon. You have to put in the miles. In order to find the courage to be vulnerable, think about the things that have helped build up your self-confidence in the past. It could be reading articles or books from your favorite authors, meeting with that sponsor or mentor who always has your back or self-reflecting on your own personal journey and realizing how far you've come. Make a list of these confidence boosters so that you can look back at it when you need a little encouragement.

You will have the courage to show up authentically and share your opinions at times and it will seem easy. Other times, when the fear of rejection is too overwhelming, you will just stand there, frozen in inaction. This will happen to you. It has happened to me and still does. However, not performing perfectly on a certain day or in a particular moment does not erase all of the preparation and miles you've put in. Your vulnerability muscle is still there. Your body remembers. Give yourself grace during the times you stumble and know that there will be another opportunity to try on vulnerability again. Believe me, those moments of deciding whether or not to show up authentically will keep coming. Just take one moment at a time.

Getting to the Point Where Your Identity Is Not a "Thing"

You'll know you have reached self-acceptance when your identity is no longer a "thing" that you are trying to hide. For me, talking freely about my family and their traditions signaled to me that I had accepted that part of myself. Even identifying myself as Latina when asked about my ethnicity was a huge milestone, as that previously brought me shame. When you are no longer worried about how others will respond to that piece of your identity you were previously hiding, this is when you will know you are now fully accepting that part of you.

We are starting to see this shift in our media. Back in the 1980s and '90s, being different from the traditional white, straight, married middle-class family often held a spotlight to it. I remember the "Puppy Episode" of the Ellen DeGeneres sitcom, *Ellen*. This was the episode when she came out. It was all anybody could talk about. It was on magazine covers, on talk shows, and it filled countless conversations around the water cooler. There were accolades and there was backlash. She even received death threats. DeGeneres's sexual orientation was a thing that everybody was discussing. I don't think many of us sit around the table and talk about the perils of being heterosexual, but being homosexual generated lots of opinions. It was a thing.

Two decades later, we are now seeing a shift, beginning in comedies such as *Schitt's Creek*. In this sitcom, David Rose, one of central characters of the story, is pansexual. What is striking about the show is that David's storyline—his dealing with his loss of wealth, his fashion, his family dynamics, his relationship with his best friend Stevie, his entrepreneurship—does not focus on his sexual orientation. Even the topic of homophobia is absent altogether. In other words, his identity, his sexual orientation, is not a "thing" that people in the show talk about. David just shows up as his himself and we experience his life through his eyes. It is small moments like these that make you feel like you are no longer an "other." That being pansexual, bisexual, homosexual or heterosexual doesn't matter. It's just part of who you are.

I am longing for the day when we don't say the "first female president" or the "first transgender CEO." When the identity is no longer the thing that we are talking about. That day will come, but only when all of us make the decision to accept all of our own wonderful, unique qualities and show up authentically with our friends, our family and at work. It is not until we can love and accept ourselves that can we expect others to accept us. The road to belonging begins with self-acceptance.

You have something of value to give to the world. Your life story and how you got to where you are today is more interesting than you realize. People want to hear about it. It might feel scary to become vulnerable and reveal aspects of the unknown you, but I can assure you that it is the best part of you. The courage to tell your story begins with believing that your story is worth telling. It begins with you believing you are enough. Once you believe you are enough, you are headed straight to the path of belonging.

MANAGER STRATEGIES

Employees, particularly people of color, are often afraid to bring their authentic selves to work. As a manager, here are a few ways you can create psychological safety so that your employees feel safe to show up authentically.

Embrace imperfection. The best managers are the ones who don't shy away from their mistakes but instead learn from them. As a leader, if you are able to be vulnerable and show your imperfection, then others around you will let go of the need to be perfect and be more willing to take risks that are good for the company.

Create a culture of trust. Be honest and transparent with your employees. If you try to hide the truth or pretend something is not happening, people always know. Creating a culture of inclusivity begins with building a culture of trust. Tell the truth, even if the truth is not pretty.

Practice active listening. When a person of color or from another underrepresented identity approaches you with their concerns about how they are feeling excluded, stop and listen. Oftentimes they are experiencing things that you are not aware of, so it may be hard for you to believe it. You may find yourself coming up with all sorts of reasons for why it is not true or how they are misinterpreting it, but remember: unconscious bias is just that—unconscious. Co-workers who treat you wonderfully may be unwittingly treating someone else poorly. It is your job to actively listen when someone shares their concerns. As a member of the Black community once told me, "Just believe us."

6

What's in Your Toolbox?

GROWING UP, I remember my dad's toolbox. It was old, rusty and always overflowing with odd-looking tools. Every time something broke in our home, he would calmly walk downstairs, look through his box and find the perfect tool. Sometimes it would take him several minutes to dig through the pile, with his head down as he carefully examined each screwdriver, hammer and wrench. Over the years, his tools began to pile up. I started to notice that, when he got new tools, he would not toss the old ones. To me, it appeared that he had duplicate sets.

When I asked my dad why he was saving one old tool, he replied, "You never know when you might need this one."

Navigating through this journey to belonging requires your own toolbox. And not just one of those shiny ready-to-go sets that you get at the hardware store when you move into your first new house. You need that old, rusty tool set that is filled with instruments of different shapes and sizes, that has been curated over many years and that you continue to add to as you progress through life. Knowing that your toolbox is right there for you when you need it gives you the confidence you need to continue forward.

When you are on the uncertain road toward self-acceptance, your tools can range from the people you decide to surround yourself with to the words you choose to say to yourself when things get hard to the communities and organizations that will support you when you feel alone. Now, let's explore some of these essential tools.

Resilience Is Your Superpower

Were you aware that resilience is a superpower? For me, this is something I learned from my parents. Growing up, I remember my parents simply doing what they needed to do to provide us with food, a nice home and a good education. They lost jobs, but then found new ones. They were treated unfairly, but they persevered. They had to take odd shifts to allow for childcare, but they did it. Every time a curveball came their way, they found a way to pivot and make it work. They didn't worry about why it wasn't fair. They just plowed ahead.

So, when I ventured off to start my own life, I had already seen what resilience looked like and was developing it myself, without even knowing it. Denied a promotion? Work harder. Invisible to leaders? Make myself irreplaceable. Not understanding the corporate culture? Find the right person to explain it to me. That was my approach. This is especially true if you are a person from an underrepresented group. Navigating life is just a little bit harder. You face more obstacles. More inequities. Less support. But you keep going, building your resilience muscle along the way.

The more I practiced resilience, the better I got at it. With every hardship, obstacle or roadblock that was put in my way, I instinctively developed a mastery of flexibility and toughness. Over time, hard things no longer fazed me.

This muscle came in handy when I returned from maternity leave after having my first daughter, Sophia. Like every new working mom, I was dreading the first day back at work. It was even more difficult because my daughter refused to take a bottle—she would only nurse. We had tried for weeks to wean her off before I had to return to work, but she would have nothing to do with it. On the night before my first day back, we called our pediatrician and asked what we should do.

"Nurse her before she goes to bed, and in the morning, don't nurse. Instead, pump, leave a warm fresh bottle for your husband, and leave for work. She will be so hungry when she wakes up and with no other option, she will take the bottle. *Don't worry. Babies don't starve themselves,*" our pediatrician assured us.

And that is exactly what we did. I woke up at 6:30 a.m., pumped, got ready for work and left. I felt confident that had I left things in good shape with a warm bottle waiting for her. Little did I know that our daughter had a different idea. My husband spent the next ten hours trying to give her the bottle while I was away at work. She refused each time, wailing with hunger. When I got home around 5:30 p.m., I was shocked to learn that my daughter had not eaten all day. We quickly called the pediatrician.

"What should we do?" we asked, exasperated. "We want to feed her, but we need to wean her from the breast."

"How long has it been?"

"Probably going on twenty hours since she's last eaten," we told him.

"What? Nurse her immediately!" our pediatrician blurted out as if we were the most incompetent parents on the planet. "I guess your baby *will* starve herself."

I could hear the shock in his voice. I'm not sure whether it was about my daughter not taking the bottle or whether it was our stupidity as new parents.

We fed her, of course, but now I had a new problem. I still had to go to work the next day. I had to somehow nurse my daughter every three hours at work until we figured out how to wean her.

I also had a new manager with a lot of hubris. He did not know me or my work so I had to prove myself yet again. The first week back at work is hard enough for any new parent, but what happened next left me numb.

"I need you to go to Brazil," my new manager informed me.

Puzzled, I asked, "When?"

"Next week," he said nonchalantly.

"What? I have never traveled in the three years I have worked here. Why do I need to travel to Brazil so urgently?"

"I'd like you to do some training."

I had never traveled to do training. I didn't understand why he would send me on a business trip during one of the most difficult transitions for a working mother. My heart dropped. It felt like a test.

How committed was I to this job?

Am I willing to do the work?

Can I work the same hours?

I carefully explained to him that my daughter would not take the bottle and would die if I left the next week. He acquiesced, but said that I needed to go as soon as possible.

At that time, I was the sole breadwinner. I needed this job, this income and these health benefits. I had no choice but to figure it out. So, we spent the next four weeks desperately trying to find a way to get my daughter to take the bottle. I didn't think twice about whether it was the best plan. I just had to do it—that resilience muscle was building without me realizing it.

Looking back at that time, I have mixed emotions. I feel anger for a manager who would put me through this painful experience. But I also feel pride for having had the strength to persevere. A decade later, this was the experience that became one of the main reasons I started a DEI program at Looker. I never wanted another young working mother to have to go through what I did.

For those of you who have had to overcome anything in your life, you have this same resilience. If you are someone who has hit the glass ceiling, been overlooked for a promotion, had to face slights or insults, been treated like you were invisible, you know exactly what it feels like to overcome. You intuitively know how to get up, try again and push forward no matter how hard it might be. That is your superpower. Often, we don't notice that we even have this tool. It's just who we are. It is what's necessary to survive. It is the secret sauce that you didn't even know you had.

We saw the power of resilience during the 2020 pandemic. Companies around the globe suddenly found themselves in emergency mode, having to overcome unimaginable crisis after crisis. What was interesting during this time was to see who navigated it the best. The *Harvard Business Review* cites a study of 454 men and 366 women who were assessed during the COVID-19 pandemic on their leadership effectiveness. The study found that, in the middle of this crisis, the women were rated more positively in thirteen of the nineteen competencies that comprise overall leadership effectiveness. Companies were in need of leaders who could pivot and learn new skills, who could empathize with employees when times are tough, who could display honesty and integrity, who were understanding of the stress, anxiety and frustration that employees were feeling. In the study, the women leaders were rated higher on all of these skills.

This combination of empathy and crisis management is nothing new to women. As women executive leaders, we have had to overcome hard things over and over again, so we know exactly what to do when an unexpected crisis shows up. Women have also traditionally been the primary caregivers at home, juggling household responsibilities and work. The struggle and hardship of managing childcare and work is not new to working moms, so they were the first to be able to pivot to at-home Zoom calls with kids around them.

If you sat down with a piece of paper and wrote out all of the scenarios that you have had to overcome over the years, you will start seeing your own pattern. You will start seeing that you do not give up. That you keep going, despite the setbacks. That no hill is too large and no challenge is too big. You just keep doing. You have *resilience* in your toolbox. Don't shrug it off like it's nothing, or assume that everyone has it. They don't. Trust me. Appreciate the strength that your resilience gives you and gain comfort from the fact that it will show up when you need it the most.

NEXT SMALL THING

Make a timeline of the major moments in your career. Write your successes above the line and mark them with a square. The greater the success, the higher you place it. Now, below the line, write down the challenges and setbacks you encountered along the way and mark them with a circle. The harder the challenge, the lower you put it.

When you are finished, take a look at your timeline and see if you notice a pattern. Does it look like a wave? Do you see periods of growth and successes following periods of struggle? What skills or qualities—like resilience—have you been nurturing all these years that will help you overcome hard things?

Find Your People

You need to find your people. Life cannot be done alone. It may work for a little while, but eventually you will doubt yourself, get overwhelmed and just be plain lonely. You need people around you who will lift you up when you are down. Folks who will remind you of your worth when you forget. And people who will accept you exactly as you are. Those people are out there, you just have to find them.

In the early part of my career, I thought I didn't need anyone. I thought I could push through things on my own. However, like a boxer, with each punch and strike your body gets weaker and weaker as the rounds go on. As I was nearing my mid-forties, I realized I had stood in that ring alone far too long and that I needed a support system. A team of people I could turn to when the doubts creeped in. Working sixty-hour weeks as a corporate lawyer while at the same time being the 100-percent committed mom and wife was an impossible standard that I had placed on myself. After years of trial and error, I found that I needed a personal champion, a true friend and a community.

YOUR PERSONAL CHAMPION

For me, my lifeline has been my husband, Derek. I know that not everyone has a partner in their life, so this is not to say that my way is better. It is just what has worked for me. Your own personal champion might be your best friend, a mentor or a family member. A therapist can also be a perfect personal champion because all they care about is you.

Since Derek and I first met in college, he has seen how hard I've had to work. He has seen the struggles placed in front of me and has seen me overcome them. As a white male, he has also noticed the disparities in how he is regularly treated versus how I am often treated. While I have practiced law for twenty-five years and he left the law after five, I can't tell you how many times people still contact him instead of me for legal advice.

Despite having worked at a well-known law firm as well as at hot Silicon Valley start-ups, I still found my confidence declining over the years. I look back at this now and realize that those constant slights at the office contributed to this feeling of being an imposter—but, as an outsider, Derek only noticed my achievements. I, on the other hand, would forget all of my achievements the second someone asked me, "What do you do?" When these moments occurred, he would be the first to remind me how accomplished I was. He would recite back to me all of the different projects I had managed, companies I had worked at, deals I had completed.

Derek had a running list in his mind of all my life's accomplishments and would rattle them back to me when I was living in self-doubt. He was my person to remind me that I was enough. That I deserved the promotion. That I was capable of being a general counsel. That I was worthy of being a board member. Find that person in your life who will point out all of your accomplishments when you seem to forget them. Find your own personal champion.

A TRUE FRIEND

Friends are essential. And not the kind of friend you try to impress with the latest fashions or fancy car. The kind you can show up to as your true messy self. The kind to whom you can tell all the mistakes you've made and the pain you are feeling and they in turn will simply listen without judgment. Those are the kinds of friends you need. Because life is hard.

I spent most of my adult life trying to impress people, not only at work but in my personal life as well. When I was a young girl, my mom would tell me to dress well so that people would know I came from a good family. She was an immigrant, and so

I understand why she felt the need to prove our worth. It was as if we had to earn our right to be a part of our community. It wasn't automatically given to us.

As a result, I was always trying to prove to new friends and colleagues that I was worthy of their friendship or acceptance. Only the shiny "perfect" me would show up. While I made friends as I went through life, I never really revealed too much. I mostly shared the good stuff with them—all the children's awards and achievements and stories of wonderful summer trips. It was very similar to the types of posts you see on social media these days. Just the happy times. I kept a safe distance and rarely revealed the hard things in the fear that I would no longer be worthy of approval. Even later, I would hold back from sharing my fears of not being smart enough at work, or how I felt like a failure as a mom.

It wasn't until I found my friend Michele that things changed. I remember the exact day I met her. We were at a local community pool where our kids were swimming one hot day. There was something about her kind tone and welcoming aura that drew me in. Instead of feeling tense and on guard, I immediately felt my body soften and relax. I remember her giving me a compliment. I don't remember what it was about, but I remember how she made me feel. Michele was different. She didn't boast about her kids or show off some new fancy purse; instead, she immediately talked about the hard stuff. How hard it was to raise kids and how balancing it all was so difficult. I felt, in that moment, that I could trust this person. What I didn't realize then was that this new friend I made at the side of a swimming pool would be that confidante who would support me through some of the hardest times in my life.

Look for friends who embrace you for your authentic self— whatever that looks like. If you feel like you have to change any part of yourself to be around a person, that is not your true friend. You want friends in your life who lift you up, celebrate your successes, cry with you during the hard times and encourage you to be yourself.

CONNECT WITH A COMMUNITY

Your community is the people with whom you feel fellowship, because you share the same interests, values and goals. It took me a long time to realize how important living in or with a community is. As immigrants, my parents worked all the time, oftentimes holding multiple jobs. They rarely relied on others for help. In order for us to always have a parent around when we came home from school, my parents worked opposite shifts: my mom worked during the normal business day and my dad worked evenings. This meant they were never home together. They selflessly put the lives of their children ahead of their own. As a result, there weren't many BBQs with friends, or much attendance at community events. It was just work, family and survival. Like my parents, I believed that I didn't need anyone. I could go at it alone.

When I was coming up through the ranks, I did it mostly alone. I was the only woman in the room and the only person of color in the room. I had no one to share my doubts or frustrations with. I also thought that my feelings of inadequacy or invisibility were only my own. It wasn't until I found women's organizations that I realized I was not alone. I started going to conferences and was surprised to learn that so many other women were feeling the same way. The simple knowledge that you are not alone—that you are part of a community—was enough. Being part of an organization that shares your beliefs and values makes you feel seen, safe and welcome. It makes you feel like you belong.

In 2020, during the middle of the pandemic, I came across an organization called How Women Lead. It was led by a passionate woman named Julie Castro Abrams. As I was getting to know her organization, I remember one particular webinar that changed my life.

No more mean girls!

I stopped what I was doing. I was multi-tasking and checking email when I heard this phrase.

No more mean girls!

Be fierce advocates for each other.

Say yes to helping each other.

These words stopped me in my tracks. They were what I had been looking for all my life. A group of executive women who wanted to lift each other up. I had found my people.

Their credo spoke to me. They talked about how things can change for women when you stop competing with each other and instead start advocating for each other. We started our Zoom meetings not by chitchatting about football or baseball, but instead by talking about menopause and reproductive rights. We all felt seen.

Finding a community where you have a shared set of values and beliefs is more important than you think. You may think your beliefs are so unique that there is no group out there for you. Or that you don't have enough time in your day to add another event to your calendar. I challenge you to explore. It may take a few tries, but I can tell you that when you find your people, you will just know, and you will realize what they can bring to your life.

SELF-REFLECTION MOMENT

- Who are the people in your life who have supported you and lifted you up along the way? Do you have a personal champion? If not, what kind of person are you looking for? List out the qualities so that you can be intentional in fostering those types of relationships.

- Examine your friendships. Are they friends that you can share the hard, messy stuff with or only the picture-perfect stuff? Think about whether these friendships are really serving you and, if they aren't, consider making a change.

- What kind of organization would you enjoy being part of? Pick an organization and attend an event. See what you think. You may be surprised how comforting it is to be around people who have a shared interest or experience.

Why Mentors and Sponsors Matter

I had never heard the term "mentor" growing up. Most first-generation professionals like me haven't. However, if you have read any leadership book, you will typically find a chapter in there about the importance of mentorship, and, more recently, the value of sponsorship. This book is no different. I cannot underscore enough how critical it is to find the people in your life who will help you achieve your goals.

Many people ask me what the difference is between a mentor and a sponsor. Simply put, mentors advise you and sponsors advocate for you. The SLAC National Accelerator Laboratory at Stanford has produced a very useful comparison for these two roles.

Mentors vs Sponsors

Mentors have mentees.	→	Sponsors have protégés.
A mentor could be anyone in a position with the desired experience who can offer advice and support to a mentee.	→	A sponsor is a senior-level staff member invested in a protégé's career success.
Mentors support mentees through formal or informal discussions about how to build skills, qualities and confidence for career advancement.	→	Sponsors promote protégés directly, using their influence and networks to connect them to high-profile assignments, people, pay increases and promotions.
Mentors help a mentee craft a career vision.	→	Sponsors help drive their protégé's career vision.
Mentors give mentees suggestions on how to expand their network.	→	Sponsors give protégés their active network connections and make new connections for them.
Mentors provide feedback to aid a mentee's personal and professional development.	→	Sponsors are personally vested in the upward movement of their protégé.
Mentors offer insight on how a mentee can increase visibility through finding key projects and people.	→	Sponsors champion their protégé's visibility, often using their own platforms and reputation as a medium for exposure.
Mentors passively share the "unwritten" rules for advancement in their organization with mentees.	→	Sponsors actively model behavior and involve protégés in experiences that enable advancement.

You need both of these roles in your life. Let me briefly describe why.

MENTORS

My first job after the law firm was with a company called Vantive as a corporate securities counsel. The general counsel at Vantive was David. David was a natural-born teacher, who often did things like institute cross-functional training for us all during our lunch hour. Whatever it was, he was always helping us expand our skillsets. The company got acquired only one short year after I started working there and I was devasted not to be able to continue to learn from him.

As the years went on, it was always David I would call when I was considering a new opportunity. Every time I reached out, despite his incredibly busy day, he would always call right back. And not just in a few days, but that same day. Without realizing it, I had a mentor.

I remember when I called to ask for his advice on whether I should take my first general counsel job. At the time, my kids were in elementary school and my life was busy. On this particular day, I escaped into my closet, the only quiet place in the house, to hold the call.

"Dave, I have an opportunity to be a general counsel. It sounds like a big job and I am not sure I am ready for it. What do you think?"

He asked a few questions about the company and my role, and then, without hesitation, he said, "You should take that job. You are absolutely ready for it."

He pointed out all the reasons why I was ready to take the job and why it would be a great step in my career. I remember sitting there in that dark closet, feeling excited about what I had just heard. Coming from David, those words mattered. I definitely had doubts on whether I could do it, but I kept remembering his words: "You are absolutely ready for it." I trusted Dave, so I forged ahead.

He was right. It was a great next step in my career. I am not sure I would have taken that leap without his support. I needed someone I respected to encourage me to go out of my comfort zone. I would often call him through the years when I needed an introduction, was stuck on a thorny issue or needed guidance on how to scale a legal department. As a first-generation professional, I did not have a network. I also did not have a parent, family member or friend who could "show me the ropes." In fact, in many cultures, women are discouraged to advance too high in their profession once they have children, so just having someone on your side is enough. As a woman of color with no network or role models to learn from, having a mentor like David gave me the confidence, knowledge and road map to progress in my career.

SPONSORS

You also need a sponsor. In some ways, sponsors are even more important. Sponsors are people who highlight your achievements and constantly look for a place you could shine. They are your advocate in the room when you are not there. They can certainly give you advice, but they do more than that. Sponsors are particularly important if you are from an underrepresented group. Having someone in your corner who can speak to your abilities and promote you into the next big project or new role can make the difference. Sponsors are the ones who think about you when such new opportunities come up. In fact, according to *Forbes*, "promotion is the core purpose of sponsorship, and in an ideal scenario, sponsors actively endorse their sponsored party and work to elevate that person's status within an organization." Sponsors are critical in helping you achieve a sense of belonging. A sponsor looks out for you. They don't just give you advice. They act.

As I reflect on my career, there was one sponsor who was pivotal. It was 2020 and we were in the middle of the pandemic. As I was thinking of what to do next in my career, I started reading the data on board representation. I was shocked to learn how underrepresented Latinas were in the boardroom. In California, Latinos make up over 40 percent of the population but Latina representation in the boardroom is miniscule. On Fortune 1000 boards only 1 percent of California seats are held by Latinas, and on the Russell 3000 Index Latinas hold less than half a percent of California board seats. Such data overwhelmingly showed that Latinas were the least represented in the boardroom and had the widest gap to close.

As a result, I wanted to join a board and start changing those statistics. I went through board readiness training, polished up my resume and created a board bio. Like with most things in my career, I knew it would be hard, but I didn't realize how hard. After about one year of networking and rejections, I felt like maybe it was not going to happen. Maybe I did not have the experience or credentials for becoming a board member. The flood of thoughts that come from imposter syndrome started to rush back.

That is when I decided to call Brooke. If you look at Brooke's pedigree and then at my background, you would be unlikely to think that he would be one of my sponsors. Brooke is an older white man who earned his BA in economics and MBA from Stanford and, in between, served as a lieutenant in the U.S. Navy. He served in a number of different finance positions, including as CFO of a public company, and then transitioned to the venture capital industry. Brooke has spent decades investing in and advising start-ups, and has served on a number of public and private different boards. He is one of those people whom everyone knows and respects. I was lucky enough to also know him.

I met Brooke when I was the general counsel of a private software company in the middle of my career. He was on the board and served on the audit and compensation committees. What struck me about Brooke was that, unlike other board members, he always treated me like an equal—like I belonged in the room.

At meetings, Brooke would often specifically turn to me and ask my opinion and engage in discourse with me about company matters. He valued my contributions. This continued for all the time that I worked with him, even beyond that role. Over the years I would periodically ask for advice and he always gave it. But, more importantly, he was my advocate even when I didn't know it.

During the interview process for my job as general counsel at Looker, one of the board members contacted Brooke, unbeknownst to me. I'm not sure what Brooke said to him, but when I walked into the interview, this particular board member told me that he had already talked to Brooke and that there was nothing more he needed to know. The job was mine if I wanted it. Having Brooke's sponsorship behind the scenes mattered.

Brooke was there again behind the scenes during the time when I was looking to join my first board. I was interviewing to join the board of Salsify and, like with Looker, one of the current board members contacted Brooke for a reference. Once again, he championed me. Someone in his position carries a ton of influence and power and he used it to lift me up behind closed doors. That is sponsorship.

In addition to helping me network, Brooke also imparted me with some much-needed confidence during my board search. During one of our conversations he said to me, "This will happen for you. You will add considerable value to many boards."

Coming from someone like him, that was all I needed to drown out the times when I started doubting myself or when recruiters told me it was going to be tough for me to get a board seat. If Brooke believed in me, then I could believe in myself.

Find your Brooke.

Finding Your Mentor or Sponsor

I recognize that I have been fortunate to have access to a network of brilliant minds to mentor and support me. If you are at the beginning of your career, you may not yet have met enough people to be able to find the right mentor or sponsor. Or, if you are mid-career or later, you may be feeling a little despair, wondering, "Why haven't I found the right mentor yet?" For all of you, I want you to know that you are not alone. Sponsors and mentors come from the most unlikely places. Oftentimes, they find you instead of the other way around. But, in order for them to find you, you must be ready. I truly believe the Buddhist saying, "When the student is ready, the teacher will appear." By reading this book and getting on the journey of self-acceptance with me, you are preparing yourself to be ready.

I became an unexpected teacher during the pandemic. One of the people my husband worked with during his dot-com start-up days was a woman named Zahra. She was a product development manager and web designer. Derek kept in touch with Zahra through the years.

Zahra is a Black woman, a daughter of a mixed-race marriage. By that point in her career, like many Black female professionals working in high tech, she had endured decades of microaggressions in the workplace and was struggling to make sense of it all. During the racial reckoning of 2020, she and I began talking over Zoom regularly. We each understood each other. Told our stories. Shed tears together. She was interested in starting a DEI program at her company but was facing the typical resistance you find when starting such a program. She felt like she was pushing a rock up a big hill. So, instead of her continuing to do it alone, we agreed that we would set up regular one-to-one meetings so that I could give her advice. We ended up meeting regularly for over a year. And we talked about a lot more than just DEI programs.

My relationship with Zahra is not something that we could have predicted. I hadn't spoken to her much over our first two decades. She was my husband's friend more than mine. We had completely different professions. We lived in different states. But yet, we found each other. She was searching for a teacher without knowing it, and I was yearning to teach.

Teachers, sponsors and mentors are waiting for you. They may not be completely obvious to you right now. You may be saying to yourself that nobody understands what you are going through. I am here to tell you that there is someone out there that understands you. Someone wants to help you and lift you up. Stick with me as we continue on your journey. Let's get you ready for your teacher.

It's Time to Start Creating Your Own Unique Toolbox

As you have read through this chapter, I hope that you were able to start thinking about what might be in your own toolbox. To start on your journey of building it out, find your personal champion, nurture authentic friendships and join a community that aligns with your interests. This support system will get you through those hard moments. Equally as important is building your professional network. Invest time in staying in touch with old colleagues. Most of my opportunities came from someone I used to work with. Finally, stay in touch with your mentor or sponsor. If you haven't spoken to them in a while, reach out and give them an update on your career (and don't forget to ask them how *you* can help them!). Just like with my dad's toolbox, you never know which tool is the one you will need at any given point. They are all important.

MANAGER STRATEGIES

Your employees need tools to support them on their journey toward self-acceptance. As a manager, here are some ways you can help your employees put together their own unique toolbox.

Establish a mentorship program at your company. Mentors are a great way for employees to learn and grow. A great example of a well-run mentorship program is the Fast Track initiative at venture capital firm First Round. This ninety-day experience pairs hundreds of tech leaders with high-potential operators, using a structured format that includes professional development sessions with subject matter experts, networking opportunities, guidance on questions to explore during one-to-one sessions and a feedback loop.

Be a sponsor. Employees often ask me, "How can I find a sponsor?" I tell them that you don't pick a sponsor, a sponsor finds you. As a leader, you have a wonderful opportunity to sponsor someone. A note of caution here. We tend to gravitate to people that are just like us. Be careful that you are not only sponsoring people who are similar to you. Employees from underrepresented groups have fewer people like them in leadership positions so have fewer opportunities for sponsorship. Find that high-potential employee, and invest in them.

Create a community. You can create a variety of communities within your company. Many companies now use applications like Slack to help create internal communities that are safe spaces where employees can share stories and resources and generally connect.

Examine your own efforts. Your employees are doing *their* work. Now, what are *you* doing to learn more about your diverse employees? What are you reading or listening to educate yourself about others who are different from you? Are you getting out of the way and giving credit to those who deserve it? Are you amplifying voices who have been historically silenced? Are you letting others speak instead of dominating the conversation? Examine your behavior.

7

When to
Choose Yourself

I N THE SUMMER of 2021, we were eagerly awaiting the start
of the "2020" Tokyo Olympics. The games had been delayed
a year due to COVID-19, and the world was excited to see the
athletes compete. I had watched women's gymnastics ever since
I was a little girl, when my dad took me to the 1984 Olympics
in Los Angeles. Every four years since, I have been glued to the
television, watching these girls flip, twist and turn all their way
to the Olympic podium.

The extra wait had made this year even more exciting and I,
like the rest of the world, was looking forward to seeing Simone
Biles win gold for the United States in every event. At the time,
Biles was considered the GOAT (Greatest of All Time) and she
was anticipated to sweep her category. It was going to be spec-
tacular, and sponsors were lining up to get a piece of her glory.

But as the first days of competition began, something weird
started to happen. Biles was uncharacteristically making errors.
She got through the qualifiers and she, along with the rest of

Team USA, advanced as expected, but not in the top spot. Then, the unthinkable happened. In the first event for the team competition, Biles experienced "the twisties" during her vault. The world later came to learn that the twisties is a temporary loss of balance awareness in the air. It not only limits a gymnast's ability to perform her incredibly difficult exercises, it is also extremely dangerous if she lands the wrong way. So, within minutes on the biggest day of her life, Biles had a decision to make. She could push through it, like we've all been taught. ("Suck it buttercup," as my then ten-year-old daughter's gymnastics coach used to tell her.) But Biles did the unthinkable. She gracefully removed herself from the competition. She did not go for the gold. Instead, she chose herself and her safety over the world's expectations. And she did this with the entire world watching her.

I'm not sure when it happens but, at some point in our life, we unknowingly decide to start choosing everyone but ourselves. We choose to keep working instead of getting some rest. We choose to do the housework instead of exercising. We choose to please others instead of ourselves. Watching Simone Biles choose herself that day started a national discussion on mental health. It reminded us that choosing ourselves over the expectations of others is okay.

You Get to Decide How Much You Want to Reveal and When

Back in Chapter 4, I described what it feels like to be the "invisible mom" at work. If you recall, I gave birth to my first daughter while working in a traditional corporate setting in a large public company. I was the sole breadwinner, so I had no choice but to return to work when my maternity leave was up.

In those early days as a new mother, what I most wanted was flexibility, but there was none. I knew I could get my job done if I worked remotely, especially if I did not have the extra burden of having to get ready for work, pump and store breast milk and commute every day. All these tasks added hours to my day that I didn't have. I heard that some women had found "flex-time" at other companies, but these opportunities were very few and far between. I would often call a legal recruiter to ask whether she knew of any jobs that were part-time or remote, and she always told me, "Not really. The most a company will give you is one day a week at home, max."

So, with not too many choices in front of me, I went back to work after a quick three months. While I did not feel good about returning to my job so soon, I also knew I was getting some great experience as well as access to a lot of opportunities could ultimately benefit my career. Therefore, I was willing to go back into the trenches to continue to advance my career. "I'm tough!" I kept telling myself. I could handle anything.

Back at work, managing my old workload while simultaneously taking care of a three-month-old at home who had colic and refused to take the bottle felt nothing short of impossible. Nursing rooms in the workplace were non-existent at the time. There were no other working parents who could provide tips or emotional support. Nobody was checking in to see how I was doing. I saw no other women in leadership who could assure me that this was in fact possible. I was alone and invisible as a new working mom. As a result, I suffered silently. My every day consisted of:

* An inconsolable baby suffering from colic

* Chafed nipples

* Exhaustion from sleep training

- The burden and sadness that comes from pumping (and dumping, when traveling)

While all of these experiences and emotions were quietly happening for me at home, I still had to show up every day at work with a smile on my face, perfectly put together with my pressed black blazer and ready to tackle the legal problems of the day. I was afraid to talk about how hard things were because I thought I would be judged for not being able to handle it. So, I kept quiet, determined that having a baby would not change my career trajectory. I did not want my peers or my boss to treat me differently. As I went from meeting to meeting solving problems and getting things done, nobody around me knew what was happening at home or to my body. And nobody asked. On the outside, I was confident, dedicated and in command of my profession. On the inside, I was barely holding it together and wanted to burst out in tears at any given moment.

It would be great if all of the environments we experience were welcoming—if we knew in our hearts that there would be no consequences or repercussions for showing up authentically. Unfortunately, not all situations are this way. Sometimes you have to make the calculated decision to stay hidden or small to preserve your status or your mental well-being. That is not to say this should be all of the time. The purpose of this book is to build the confidence you need so that you can depart from that way of thinking. But I also want to give you the permission to take it slowly. I want to free you of any potential shame you may feel for making the difficult choice to hide when you need to. It is okay to make the decision to show up authentically when you are ready. On your timeline. It does not have to be today.

Back in 2003, when I returned to work after the birth of my first daughter, my choices were limited. While I certainly could have elected to come back to work and publicly display my new parenthood, unabashedly talking about no sleep and chafed nipples and bravely asking for flexibility, this also would have required the backbone to endure the backlash from that decision, including the risk of being pushed out. In that moment, I knew I did not have the emotional strength for that battle. I knew it would be too hard.

Finding the Right Fishbowl

Part of the journey toward achieving a sense of belonging is determining which settings will embrace the real you and which will not. In a speaking event hosted by Terri Givens, Rosetta Lee, a diversity speaker and trainer, provided a great analogy to help determine whether an environment is well-suited for us. She compared the workplace to a fishbowl. A fishbowl is a great environment for fish. Fish enjoy water and swimming. But what happens when we add rabbits and birds to the fishbowl and don't change the environment? Birds like to fly and rabbits like to hop. Neither can swim, but we can put them in a fishbowl and ask them to thrive with all the other fish. When the rabbits and birds start struggling, we ask ourselves why they aren't thriving when all the other fish seem to be doing fine. The answer is not hard to figure out. Rabbits and birds don't swim. The environment—the fishbowl—was never adapted to meet their needs .

Corporate cultures are like fishbowls. We ask people who are different from the rest to change who they are so that they can swim along with everyone else. People placed in these situations can try and try and try, but, ultimately they do not have gills, and no matter how determined they are to swim, they will get exhausted and drown. They will drown not because they didn't want to succeed in that environment. They will drown because the environment was never set up for them to succeed.

As managers and leaders, we have a responsibility to be aware of the environment we are creating and make sure that it supports all people. But, as an individual, what can you do if that environment does not currently exist for you?

Knowing your surroundings will help you gauge whether or not it is safe enough to reveal your authentic self. First, take a look around and examine your environment. Do you find yourself in a fishbowl, or in a terrarium that was built to accommodate differences? Are there rocks or structures above the surface for you to climb up and get air or can you only survive if you have gills? If you find yourself in a fishbowl with no gills and no structures to get you out of the water, do you have managers, allies, leaders or employee resource groups that you can go to for support? Assess whether you have the option to move to another, more hospitable environment (for example, maybe another department or a different role) if you realize you are not in the right place. If you need to stay in the fishbowl for financial or other reasons, then simply notice and acknowledge the environment that you are in. Notice that it is not set up for you to succeed and that this is not within your control. Eventually, you will need to make a change. Make a plan to improve your situation slowly, whether that is to seek help within your organization or to set the wheels of change in motion by connecting with recruiters. Eventually, you will run out of air if you stay in the same situation, so you need to have a plan.

NEXT SMALL THING

Take a moment to write down what your ideal work environment would look like. Which characteristics are must-haves and which are nice-to-haves? For example, must it be remote-first or in-person? Is there a specific title or role? Ideal compensation structure? Does it require diverse leadership or a robust DEI program? Simply write down all the things you would want in your dream workplace. As you look for your next position or role within your company, be intentional on finding the job that meets these requirements. You deserve to be in the right terrarium.

Knowing When to Protect Yourself

Revealing is something that has been hard for me. My fear of being thought of as "less than" has always overpowered my desire to tell the truth. My fear is real. It stems from half a century of messages I have received. When everyone around you tells you that you are not worthy, you eventually believe it. These messages started for me as a child, when I was told not to tell my friends where we came from; reinforced by Hollywood, who told me my name was not American enough; and then continued through school, where I would sit quietly by and listen to my classmates joke about Hispanic janitors and housekeepers. I endured it in the workplace when I heard colleagues complain about the inequities of diversity mandates but yet saw no one who looked like me in positions of leadership.

Even today, when many of us believe that times are progressing, the messages continue. Raising my teenagers in a predominantly white community meant that I was regularly hearing remarks about the unfairness of affirmative action during the college application process. The parents at my daughter's school would complain about how unfair it was that their children could not check the ethnicity box as if it was some golden ticket unfairly given to Black and brown people on a perceived even playing field. Recently, one parent said this to me: "My son just read to me one of the questions on the college application. It asks him to describe something he has had to overcome in his life. He hasn't had to overcome anything. So just because he had a good life and family, he gets screwed in the college application process. This is so unfair."

I sat there, dumbfounded, not knowing how to respond to this statement. As these types of conversations unfold around us, it is no surprise that we might choose to hide our identities in any given circumstance. In some cases, we may stay quiet to avoid repercussions on our chances for advancement at work, but in many cases, it is simply to protect our mental health. We are trying to protect ourselves from the emotional toll it might take to try to educate others about what it feels like when you are not part of the majority. What it feels like to be followed in a store when you are a Black person. What it feels like when you are mistaken for the housekeeper when you are a brown person. What it feels like when everyone acts surprised to hear that you are an executive and have a doctorate instead of being the secretary. It is in those moments when having someone on your side, an ally who can step up and make the case instead of you, can really make a difference.

I saw the power of allyship during one of my daughter's soccer games. We had spent several recent weekends in a row at all-day tournaments, and for this particular tournament we had traveled to another state. We had a string of games ahead of us, and we were all pretty tired. If you've never been to one of these competitions, you need to know that your day usually starts around 6 a.m. and lasts for what feels like twelve or more hours.

As the next game started we sat down with the other parents to watch, and one of the moms started up a conversation about colleges. She led with her frustrations about how unfair it was that her older children did not get into the college of their choice because they were white. She felt like they had been passed over because they could not benefit from affirmative action programs. As I sat and listened to her share her complaint, my entire body tensed up. My chest tightened, my fingers curled up in a fist and I think I even stopped breathing for a moment. Her words triggered me. The little Latina girl inside of me who had always questioned her worth all these years shriveled up inside. I knew that I had checked that box decades earlier and all my insecurities of not achieving success on my own merit came rushing up to the surface. I also felt the pain for the next little Black or brown girl who was full of excitement about starting her college career and was sadly going to have to face this same reality all too soon. Sitting there, looking at this parent, I realized I just couldn't do it. I couldn't try to explain to her how her words were hurting me and the impact they would have on the next generation of kids. I was simply too exhausted.

Even though I had been "doing the work" on advancing racial justice over the last several years and no longer felt ashamed to speak up, I just couldn't have this conversation again. I was emotionally drained, and couldn't explain one more time to one more person about racial injustice and the inequities in our system. I couldn't endure the eye roll and resistance to the idea that there is such a thing as white privilege. I must not have much of a poker face because, within a few moments, my husband Derek went in headfirst for this hard conversation. He must have seen the scorn in my face as she was speaking, and noticed that I did not engage in the battle but instead chose to quietly shrink in my seat and lean away. I chose to be quiet.

But this time, staying quiet was not the result of fear. This time I had made a very intentional decision to protect myself. It is in these times when having an ally is critical—when there is another person in the room who has the emotional space to take on the hard conversations and who is not as emotionally invested in the outcome. On that day, I was lucky enough to have Derek at my side. He came in and picked up some of the heavy load I had been carrying for some time. He had also been "doing the work" with me over the previous several years and as a result was now more aware how those words would hurt me. He decided to take on this particular battle, even though it was not risk-free. These parents had been business clients of his, so challenging them could come at a cost. It would have been much easier for him to smile and keep quiet. But he didn't.

He explained to her about white privilege and the opportunities families like theirs enjoy for being white and wealthy. He talked about the obstacles that members from underrepresented communities have in their daily life that are absent in their life. She pushed back but Derek didn't mind. He kept addressing each point with more data for her to think about. I don't think he changed her mind that day. I am not sure whether he even made a dent in her thinking, but that wasn't the point. The point was that he continued the good fight on my behalf. He shouldered some of that burden for me and allowed me to take a break. He did not let that incident go unchallenged. That is what allyship looks like.

Unfortunately, not all of us always have an ally. I have found myself in many situations when there is no one around to take the burden off me. In those times, my immediate reaction is that it is up to me. *If I don't do it, who will?* In such moments, you have to make a choice. I am here to tell you that choosing yourself is okay. You can choose to be quiet and let that statement or action go unchallenged if you are not up for debating it. Those from underrepresented groups are the ones who usually have the emotional burden of correcting microaggressions. Doing this all the time, sometimes daily or even hourly, is exhausting. It will eventually take a toll on your mental health if you don't take breaks. Realize that not every battle is yours. Give yourself permission to take some space and rest and recover. Don't worry, you will be back. It matters too much to you.

This Work Is Hard—Be Kind to Yourself

If you are from an underrepresented group, you have likely had to pay an inclusion tax. According to Dr. Tsedale Melaku, this tax is the "time, money and mental and emotional energy required to gain entry to and acceptance from traditionally white and male institutional spaces." This is an unspoken tax. For those of us from underrepresented groups, we know we have paid this tax, we just haven't had a word for it.

If you have had to hide part of your identity during your life, you know all too well how exhausting it can be and what this inclusion tax feels like. It is not a physical exhaustion that you notice right away, like when you run a few miles or finish a workout. With exhaustion like that, your calves will be stiff or your biceps will feel like jelly, and others may even express empathy if they see you experiencing that kind of physical pain or injury. But the exhaustion you feel from hiding is unseen. You yourself may not even see it in the moment, and you may not realize that it has been building for years. Nobody asks whether you are okay because they don't see you physically crouched over in pain. You suffer in silence. Until, one day, someone says something or you witness something that makes your entire body hurt. The emotional pain eventually becomes a physical pain. It's like your mind says, "Enough! If you can't realize that you are suffering, I will force you to!" You eventually realize that you can no longer take it anymore. You can't hide any longer. You are not going to laugh off misguided jokes anymore. You are unwilling to change who you are to fit in. You are at your breaking point.

So, what can you do about it?

The first thing to do is to simply acknowledge that you have been running a marathon your whole life without realizing it. You haven't been grabbing the cups at the water station. You haven't stepped to the side of the course to walk for a bit, and you haven't replenished your body with electrolytes. You've just kept running, without nutrients, support or rest. At some point, your body will eventually tell you that you need to take a break. When that time comes, listen to that signal. Take the time you need to replenish your confidence and self-worth so that you have the strength to keep going. You will need to have that rest to continue the journey to self-acceptance.

Resting is not easy for some of us. For me, as a perfectionist, it was especially difficult. I was constantly trying to please others, and taking a break from accomplishing the next thing in my never-ending to-do list felt like I was letting others down, especially myself. I wanted to rest, but I came up with hundreds of reasons why it was not possible. I felt like I was somehow different from every other busy person out there and that I *really* didn't have time. I would say things like:

"When I finish the chores, I will get some rest."

"When I finish catching up on email, I will go out and get some exercise."

"When I have more time, I will see my friends."

Here's the secret. That time to take care of yourself is *now*. Not later today, or tomorrow or next week. Chores will never go away. There is always more email and to-dos on your list. In fact, that list often seems to get longer with each day, week or month that passes. If you wait until everything is done—until the house is clean, your email box is caught up—you will never get to you.

Like many ah-ha moments in my life, this one occurred for me in my therapist's office. Deb and I were talking about all the things I was dealing with in my life, and I was telling her that I could not understand why it was so difficult for me to juggle it all, or why I was feeling exhausted. I was on the brink of a collapse; I could feel it.

"Deb, I used to be able to handle all of this and I was fine," I said. "Why is this so hard now?"

"When was it easy for you?" she asked.

I thought about this and tried to find a time when things hadn't felt too difficult. Even at a young age I remember feeling overwhelmed at times, but I was always able to handle things. I had never felt broken like this before.

So Deb had me do an exercise. She asked me to compare my current life situation to a time when I was younger, and had me draw circles to help me see it with more clarity. I decided to pick the time of my life when I was in college. While I remember all the late nights studying, in general life, my memory of college was pretty good and felt carefree. My circles looked something like this:

Then, Deb asked me to draw the circles of my life today: one for every item that I felt responsible for and that needed my attention every day.

Circle after circle, they kept adding up until there were *a lot* of circles. I could have kept drawing, but Deb finally stopped me. The point was made. Now, my circles looked something like this:

Seeing all those circles looking back at me, it became very apparent why I felt so tired and depleted. I had not realized that, with every passing year, my circles were slowly adding up, one after another. And it never seemed like a circle ever got taken away. Some seemed so small, but weighed so much—like the pressure of deciding what was for dinner every day. My rows of circles didn't even take into account all of the additional things I could add to represent the energy I was spending on code-switching, coping with microaggressions or handling workplace bias.

When I finished the exercise, one circle was noticeably missing. The Me circle. I did not have circles representing Nap, Hike, Meditation, or Coffee with Friends because I wasn't doing any of those things. That's when I knew I needed to change things. What about you? What do your circles look like?

SELF-REFLECTION MOMENT

- Get some paper and draw a circle for each thing that you consider your responsibility: at work, at home, in your family, for your community, and so on. Don't edit it to make it look reasonable, just draw all of your circles. Be honest.

- Take a moment to look at your circles. Pause and take a deep breath, and honor that part of you that works so hard on a daily basis to keep things moving in the right direction. Take a moment to thank yourself for all that you are juggling. You are doing an amazing job at keeping it all together.

- Now ask yourself: Are there any self-care circles in your mix? Do you have circles for meditation, yoga class, naps or walks? If you have none, think about what self-care circles you would like to add.

- What circles do you want to drop? There is a great book by author Tiffany Dufu called *Drop the Ball*, in which she offers step-by-step instructions on how to reevaluate expectations, shrink your to-do list and meaningfully engage the assistance of others—freeing the space you need to flourish at work and to develop deeper, more meaningful relationships.

Making self-care a priority was the amazing result of this circle exercise. I saw that the ME circle was in jeopardy. If I did not attend to that circle, all of the others would crumble around me. Realizing this helped shift my thinking away from the belief that taking care of myself was selfish to understanding that taking care of myself benefited those around me. If I was healthy and in good shape, then I would have the energy to sign-up for carpool, attend a work event, volunteer at church, help my mother, go on a date with my husband and cheer on my daughter at her sports games without checking my email. I had to truly believe that investing in my own self-care was not only important for me, but also for those I loved.

Taking the First Step to Choosing Yourself

Step one is to figure out what the first step is. Your first step might be different from someone else's first step. My first step is not the same as your first step. There may also be multiple first steps. There is no right or wrong here. It is just your first step.

What is the thing that you are depriving yourself?

What is the one small change you could make in your life that might improve your day-to-day?

Where could you use more support?

What is one thing that you could take out of your life that is not serving you?

Once you figure out your first step, then you pull out one of the tools I introduced in Chapter 6—small steps, repeated often—and start there. For me, I had multiple first steps. I had to fix my hip to remove the excuse that I can no longer run and get exercise. I also had to make getting enough rest a promise I wouldn't break. Go to bed earlier or take a guilt-free nap. Another step for me was making a commitment to start saying no to things that I didn't want to do. This was a hard one because I did not want to disappoint anyone. Finally, I had to learn how to lean into vulnerability and admit that I had to work through years of marginalization and feelings of unworthiness, and seek a therapist to help me through those hard discoveries.

Each of these steps by themselves were hard. They did not happen overnight. Some were easier, like choosing to take a nap on Sunday. I just simply started doing it. Some took weeks or months, like getting physical therapy twice a week on my hip. And some took years, like unpacking all of the baggage of my past through therapy.

The important point is that you have to start. Start somewhere. If you take the actions in this chapter, eventually your body will tell you when it is replenished and ready to move on. All of sudden, things won't seem quite as hard. Tasks will become easier. Your purpose will become clearer and your spirit will get rejuvenated. Once that happens, you are ready to start removing the mask that has kept you hidden, and start moving toward showing up as your authentic self.

MANAGER STRATEGIES

Striving for perfection, trying to fit in and/or advocating for workplace equity takes a major toll on an employee's mental health. Here are some steps you can take to support your employees' well-being.

Don't place the entire burden of DEI on your underrepresented employees. This group tends to be the ones that step up first because they are the most impacted, but this is the exact demographic you are trying to support. By trying to run a DEI program "on the side," these employees jeopardize their ability to succeed, or to take on stretch projects. Instead, invest in a dedicated person to run your DEI programs.

Be an ally. Allyship is a verb. It requires action. It is not just talking about workplace equity, it is actively interrupting bias, and advocating for the underrepresented when they are not in the room. To help spread this understanding, offer allyship training that provides your managers with the tools they need to show up as an effective ally.

Talk openly about mental health. Mental health issues still have tremendous stigma and employees may feel reluctant to ask for help. The more managers talk about their own bouts of struggle, the more employees can be honest about theirs. Consider mental health breaks that apply to your *entire* group or organization, rather than forcing individual employees to ask for them. For example, you could launch "no-meeting Fridays" or "no-meeting lunch hours."

Support employees on medical leave. If an employee needs to take medical leave for things such as a mental health issue, elder care, or the loss of a loved one, they are going through a lot. Consider giving them paid time off so that they can attend to these matters without added financial stress. When they return, check in to see what kind of support they need to transition back to work, such as fewer hours at first. In the end, your employees simply want to feel seen and heard. If you can be there for them in their darkest hour, they will reward you with loyalty and commitment.

8

Hiding Only Serves You for So Long

I T WAS SUNDAY, June 28, 2020. Dr. Gena Cox had decided to watch the BET Awards, a ceremony that celebrates African American achievements in music, sports, television and movies. Gena doesn't typically watch these types of award shows, but she decided to stay up late that night anyway. George Floyd had been killed just a short month before, and, as a Black woman, Gena wanted to share this moment with other African Americans. Within a few minutes of the start of the show, a thirteen-year-old gospel singer named Keedron Bryant started to sing a song called "I Just Wanna Live." Gena sat there in her home, glued to the television as he sang the lyrics. In the song, Keedron talks about being a young Black man walking around not wanting any trouble but feeling like prey. He just wants to live. *He just wants to live.*

Gena unexpectedly burst out into tears. Not just a few tears that slowly roll down your face, but inconsolable crying that takes you to your knees. She cried for about twenty minutes, sometimes so hard that she was sliding off her chair. It was in that moment that Gena decided she could no longer hide. It was no longer an option.

Dr. Gena Cox had earned her PhD in industrial/organizational psychology and spent twenty years advising and coaching leaders on organizational change. Ever since she started her career, she was the only one in the room—the only woman and the only Black person. She had learned early on in her career what it took to be a successful Black woman in corporate America and played the part flawlessly. She straightened her hair and wore perfectly fitted suits to work every day. She was very formal in her communications and style. She believed that if she looked and acted the part, she would advance. But the opposite happened. Gena was not getting the invitations or promotions that others around her received. She was "accidentally" left out from meetings. Ironically, by trying so desperately to fit in, she had made herself invisible. She was left sitting alone on the sidelines, looking in.

Sitting on that floor on the evening of the 2020 BET Awards, Gena realized that playing the corporate part and not being herself no longer served her or others around her.

In telling me her story, she recalled the moment:

I said to myself, Gena, you are so fake. You advise leaders on how to build inclusive cultures and how to be more effective leaders, but your own personal experience has never been that.

In that moment, everything changed for Gena. She realized that that she had not used her knowledge or influence to address the real problems in the workplace. She told me she "came out" that evening as a Black woman. She quit her job and forged a new path. Gena knew that hiding no longer served her.

When Hiding Your Authentic Self No Longer Works

People hide in so many different ways. Some of us hide behind a name. We think that by simply getting rid of or shortening that ethnic-sounding name we will blend in easier. Others may stay silent about their same-sex marriage. Some may conceal their learning disability by relying on technology or team members. If you are a light-skinned Black or brown person, you may quietly enjoy the privileges of passing as white. It can be a big thing or a little thing. I was surprised to learn that even Gena, a Black woman, was hiding from her Black identity. While she couldn't hide her skin color, she did straighten her hair and wear conservative suits to hide behind a curtain of corporate formality.

Hiding any part of yourself will deprive you of living your best life. You will be devoting energy to concealing things rather than creating things. For me, I hid behind my light skin, straightened hair and American name to erase my ethnic background and I hid the battle wounds of being a working mom from my male colleagues to be part of the group. I felt like I needed to hide certain parts of my identity to thrive in the environment of corporate America. Many people hide their identity to conform to the majority, but few talk about it because it is too shameful. For those who are first-generation professionals, like me, your immigrant parents likely taught you to work hard, blend in and not rock the boat. It works for a while, but eventually it all collapses.

Hiding Can Lead to Deep Feelings of Shame

When you have spent years, even decades, hiding something about yourself, you are likely drowning in feelings of shame. Why? Because if you are hiding something it means you do not believe that you are good enough just the way you are.

This was the case for Tammy Ramos. Tammy is an expert in diversity, equity and inclusion and is currently the executive director of LatinaVIDA, an organization that partners with Fortune 500 companies to provide leadership development programs and coaching designed to empower Latina executives to advance their careers. Tammy earned her JD from Notre Dame Law School and her bachelor of science in economics and business administration with a double major in Spanish from Saint Mary's College of California. Tammy's list of accolades is long and admirable, but the road to her success was riddled with obstacles and heartache.

Tammy was the first in her family to graduate from high school. She was born to a sixteen-year-old girl who was a high school dropout. Tammy's father quickly left her mom when he learned of the pregnancy because he was afraid to be deported.

Later, her mother married a white man, who became Tammy's stepfather. Her mother had three more kids who were all fair skinned, unlike Tammy. Her half-sister had red hair and green eyes, her half-brother had blond hair and blue eyes and her other sister, while having brown hair and brown eyes, was fair skinned. Growing up in this blended family, Tammy clearly stood out with her dark skin, dark eyes and dark hair. Her ethnicity was obvious all the time. She hated being brown and she hated being Mexican. She wanted so desperately to be white so she could fit in with her siblings, her family and her community.

As a young person, Tammy often fantasized about being white. She considered coloring her hair, getting green contacts and lightening her skin. She definitely did everything she could to stay out the sun so she wouldn't tan further. When they were out in public, people asked whether she was adopted because of how different she looked from the rest. As a result, Tammy learned early in life to hide her "Latinidad." All she wanted was to be accepted and to belong.

Once, when she was a teenager, one of Tammy's white uncles told her that "Mexicaness" is garbage—but not to worry because he didn't look at her that way. His intent was not to cause her harm, but it did. He was trying to tell her that the family loved her *despite* being Mexican, but his words penetrated deeply, leaving her feeling inferior, like something was inherently wrong with her. If only she weren't Mexican, maybe then she'd be worthy of love and respect. These words would haunt Tammy for years to come.

As Tammy moved on to college and law school, she not only continued to downplay her ethnicity, she also hid the fact that she had been a foster child. Tammy had grown up in severe poverty, abuse and neglect while everyone around her seemed to have grown up in stable, affluent and loving families. Her classmate's parents were professionals such as lawyers, doctors, and politicians. Tammy's parents were not. She was very embarrassed and didn't want them to know about her poor Mexican family history because she wanted them to think she was like them. She wanted to belong, to fit in, to be accepted. She was scared that if people knew she had lived in an orphanage and came from meager beginnings, they would think she was a fraud, a counterfeit, someone who didn't deserve to be in their circles, certainly not at a top-tier law school.

When she graduated law school, she went to work at a firm where she was one of two women and was the only person of color. Again, she did the same things to try to fit in. Through school and her early professional career, Tammy simply wanted to have a sense of belonging.

It has taken a long time for Tammy to be proud of her Latinidad, of her dark brown skin and of being Mexican. But now she finds beauty in the Latino community and has dedicated her life to it. Like for me, Tammy's realization was a slow one. It was an accumulation of a lifetime of not being accepted and of gradually realizing that hiding that part of the story wasn't worth it anymore.

I have had those same feelings of shame. For me, I felt guilt for having made it to the top of my profession without identifying proudly as a Latina in the workplace. It almost seemed to me that I had achieved such great success *despite* being Latina. In fact, because of the backlash against programs such as affirmative action, I felt I needed to prove that I earned my success solely on my merits and not because of some diversity mandate. To pass as white for most of my career filled me with shame. I was embarrassed that I had not said anything. Very few Latinas make it to the top ranks of corporate America, so why did I not stand proud to be Latina? How could I not represent my community? The answer is actually quite easy. There was no one around me who looked like me. I felt like I had too much to lose early in my career to do anything different.

Hiding eventually takes a toll on your mental health, because while you are staying quiet an essential part of who you are is being devalued. In an article in *Oprah Daily*, Dr. Tina Opie, an associate professor in the management division at Babson College, said this:

> Think of aspects of your identity as buckets. Say I have a "woman" bucket that's full to the brim—a huge part of my sense of self is about being female, and I seek out opportunities to express myself in that way. Yet in my workplace, I receive constant feedback that women are not valued, so I feel the need to alter how I behave and how I present myself. I find myself carrying this heavy "woman" bucket and trying to hide it at the same time. Such circumstances can create a powerful sense of cognitive dissonance—in this case, the psychological discomfort that comes with having one value while being rewarded for acting in opposition to it—that is compounded over time. The hiding can lead to shame. You become upset with yourself because you think you're not proud or courageous enough to stand up to people who are devaluing a key part of your identity. The longer this goes on, and the more essential the part of yourself you feel forced to deny, the more your mental health can suffer.

For many of us, the racial reckoning of the summer of 2020 was the moment we could no longer play a different part. The killings of George Floyd, Breonna Taylor and Ahmaud Arbery were a wake-up call. The social climate changed so drastically in America. Those of us from underrepresented communities always knew that racism, sexism, homophobia and all the other biases existed, but we had somehow become accustomed to the normalcy of it. Oddly, most of us were comfortable with it because it was the only thing we knew. According to a study of 1,700 workers commissioned by *Modern Health* and conducted by Forrester Research, 63 percent of managers and 57 percent of employees felt affected by the major events of ongoing racism following 2020, but also felt they had to leave it out of their work life. But in the summer of 2020, similar to Gena, many decided that they could no longer hide. The benefits of hiding no longer outweighed the pain of staying quiet.

My first step toward leaning into authenticity was during the preparation for my interview for the general counsel position at Looker. When I decided to take that interview, I made a very intentional choice to show up as myself, curly hair and all. It was the most authentic version of myself that I thought I could be at the time. I decided to show up as more of me and less of the corporate part I had played for so many years. That meant dumping the formal black blazer, white collared shirt and suit pants that had been my go-to interview attire for decades and replacing them with jeans, a bright-colored blouse and a casual jacket. I was okay if I was not accepted. If there wasn't "a cultural fit," as people would often say, I didn't care. I had decided that I no longer had the energy to put on the masquerade, or to turn myself into a pretzel to fit in to a certain environment. At that point, I found little benefit in hiding and the energy, pain and shame of being something I was not was no longer bearable. When you notice in yourself that you can no longer carry that burden, that it costs too much to gain approval from others, then you will know that you are on the road toward self-acceptance.

Uncovering Your True Self May Take a Few Tries

As you go through this journey toward self-acceptance, you may notice that there are layers of uncovering. One day you may think you have fully arrived as the true you, and then realize later that you were still keeping things about your identity a secret.

Unknowingly, you had put up additional walls to protect your-self. That's okay. Uncovering your true self may take a few tries.

As I look back at my journey toward self-acceptance, while I am proud of that pivotal moment of interviewing with my natu-ral hair and casual style at Looker, I realize that, even back then, it wasn't truly my authentic self. It was only Tricia version 1.0. I did not appreciate that eradicating decades of hiding was going to be a slow process. During that interview I did a few small things to show up differently, but I had not yet fully embraced all of me. If I am being honest, I probably still haven't embraced it. Little by little I continue to learn more about myself. It's like a great awakening. The day I started talking about my family in Ecuador and El Salvador moved me from Tricia version 1.0 to 1.5. The decision to stop straightening my hair gently moved me from Tricia 1.5 to 2.0. Regularly interrupting bias and challeng-ing assumptions no matter the personal consequence moved me from Tricia 2.0 to 2.5. I can't imagine what version 5.0 of Tricia might look like!

NEXT SMALL THING

Think about the version of "you" that is showing up at work today. Write down what that version looks like. It's okay if you are still in hiding or starting at version 1.0. Don't judge it. Just study it so you know where your starting point is.

Now, look ahead to the future and write down what your version 5.0 might look like. What are the physical characteristics? What are you wearing? What are you sharing about yourself? How comfortable are you with the new you? What communities are you part of? Create a vision of what this new version of "you" might look like so you have something to aspire to.

You Don't Have to Be Accepted by Everyone

Your true self will not be accepted everywhere. Part of the journey is finding those places and people that accept you exactly as you are. The first time I felt this sense of belonging was in the oddest place—law school. But not at first. I had to search for it.

I went from a very large public university where I was just a number to a small, private Jesuit law school where everybody knew everybody. When I applied, I did not consider what going to a small private law school would feel like. I assumed it would not be much different from college. When I arrived, I realized how different it was.

I came to the first day excited to begin. I had packed my clothes, my law books and a few essential toiletries. I had to pay for my tuition and books with student loans, so there was not much money left over for niceties. I remember walking into my new apartment and meeting my roommate for the first time. She was beautiful and perfectly put together with the latest fashion. She walked around with an air of confidence. And she had lots of stuff. I mean *lots* of stuff. She had a new plush down comforter, decorations for the wall, a closet full of designer clothes and shoes and even a brown fancy stepping stool for climbing into her beautifully decorated queen-size bed. Her room and my room looked drastically different. I had some new sheets and a comforter but I don't remember whether they matched. No designer clothes. No fancy shoes and no wall decorations. I didn't even know some people used stepping stools to get into their bed.

I immediately felt *lesser*, at least as compared to her. It was clear to me that she came from a wealthy family and that she certainly was not taking out student loans like I was. As I met other law students on campus, I realized that this was the case for many. My classmates included sons of real estate moguls, daughters of CEOs and even the son of a member of the House of Representatives. I was the daughter of two immigrants who spoke with broken accents and held ordinary jobs. Like Tammy's experience in law school, I did not immediately feel like I belonged in this institution.

After a few days at school struggling to gain the confidence I needed to adapt to this new environment, I came across the Academic Success Program (ASP) that supported underrepresented students. ASP was designed to help students develop the skills they needed to succeed in law school. I signed up immediately. I knew I needed all the help I could get. In this program I met other law students who felt the same way I was feeling, so I started to feel a little better.

During the first year of law school, students often form study groups to support each other through exams, so that is what I did. My first-year study group consisted of a mix of different people: Black, Latino, Asian American and Pacific Islander, Jewish, LGBTQ+ and me. I never thought then about how different we all were, but as I look back and reflect on where I felt the most accepted in my life, this study group comes to the top of my mind. While we all came from different backgrounds and lived experiences, we all had one thing in common. We were all *others*. Each of our families had worked hard to give us a good education and had put their dreams on our shoulders. We were all carrying the heavy weight of what our success would mean to our families. None of us came from great wealth, so we all watched every penny because we knew we had to pay it all back someday. It was a place where I could show up scared, vulnerable and overwhelmed and there was always someone there to lift me up. We would come to this group seeking help and would give help in return. If one of us was falling behind, it was our mission as a group to catch them up. I don't know how I would have made it through law school without them. We all graduated, passed the bar and went on to have amazing careers. From this group, we now have several law firm partners, high-tech attorneys and a judge.

What I remember most about this group is that I did not have to pretend. When they met my family, they would tell me how they adored my parents and their accents. Some of them would even speak Spanish with them. I never worried about what I was wearing or what car I was driving. Those things didn't matter. We laughed, hugged and cried together. We shared different ethnic cuisines from each other's cultures and we learned new celebrations we hadn't celebrated before. We were just ourselves and we enjoyed each other for exactly who we were. That is when you know you belong. When you are exactly who you are. When you don't have to change a thing and you are celebrated for it.

You Now Have a Choice to Make

When the benefits of hiding no longer outweigh the pain of keeping part of you hidden, you will be forced to make a decision.

In the process of writing this book I interviewed several business leaders, including CEOs, C-suite executives and board members. Most were women or people of color, largely because these groups have a lot more at stake in the workplace and as a result are more likely to hide something about themselves to advance. The common theme among all of them was the belief that to be successful at work they needed to hide that piece of their identity that was not part of the dominant group. For those who have reached the other side, there is also another common theme. That it is too exhausting to keep up the charade. The shame, guilt, embarrassment and all the myriad feelings that come from hiding are too heavy a burden to carry.

What to Do When You Are Rejected

There will be times when you will go out on a limb and put yourself out there and you will be rejected. This can be crushing. You may even be saying to yourself that it is not worth it, thinking that if you present as your authentic self at work or in your community, then you will risk losing a job, missing out on a promotion or losing friends. That you are not willing to make that sacrifice.

I wish I could tell you that it will all work out if you decide to show up as your authentic self. That if you muster up all the courage in the world and do all the things I tell you to do, you will be welcomed with open arms and find a happily ever after. But I can't tell you that. I don't know that for sure. In some cases, you will have the happily ever after, and in some cases you won't. What is important is whether you have the tools to manage the times when there is not a happy ending.

Deciding to show up as your authentic self requires you to think about the potential consequences of being rejected. When I was a young working parent and the sole breadwinner in an all-male and toxic environment, I felt like I had no choice but to hide and go along with things. If I had shown up authentically, I would likely have been pushed out of the job. At the time, I could not have handled losing my job. So I give you permission to forgive yourself if you are currently in a similar situation. I hope that my book will help you along the journey so that one day you have the tools to leave it, but it may take time and that's okay.

Other times in life, losing a promotion, a job or even social status will be worth it. I recently made that choice. We live in a small, predominantly white, close-knit community. After the racial reckoning of 2020, our families from underrepresented identities formed a group and started to voice their concerns about the bullying and racism that existed in our community. I knew I had to help this group because I held a position of privilege and influence in our town. I spent about two years working with community leaders to try to improve the situation. While we made some progress, it was slow and was met with a lot of resistance. In 2022, a sophomore in our local high school sadly took his own life. He was a Latino boy who had been previously bullied at school. Something ignited in my body that told me I could not stay quiet anymore. Change was happening too slowly, which ultimately cost this boy his life. I decided to write an op-ed piece in our local newspaper asking our community to self-examine their unconscious bias. I knew as I wrote the piece that it would not be well-received by certain people. My husband was mayor at the time, and we were prominent and well-respected members of our community, so I knew it would cause tensions. We lived in a community that desired peace and harmony and many were not ready to have these uncomfortable conversations. I did it anyway. I knew the risks—losing friends, losing social status and being treated differently—but it was worth it.

As I suspected, there was backlash. Some community leaders intimated that I was creating division in our community. Others told me that racism, bullying and discrimination did not exist in our town, despite facts to the contrary. All of these comments were very difficult to listen to. On the other hand, hundreds of others came forward—many behind the scenes, still living in fear—to support me. They thanked me for having the courage to expose the problem. Others thanked me for providing a perspective they had never thought of before and told me that they would begin to do their own self-reflection. That particular feedback was the best. My goal was to move this community along in its journey and I was doing that one by one. I had friends and family that supported me when I felt alone. I had the tools to manage the negative self-talk when it showed up. And I had my DEI communities and resources to remind me that I was doing the right thing.

Rejection is not easy. It is how we respond to rejection that is the key. If you have made or are about to make the difficult decision to show up as your authentic self and you are worried about the consequences of rejection, here are some strategies to help you manage it:

- Reach out to a friend, family member, mentor, or therapist who accepts you exactly as you are and ask for their support.

- Seek out groups within your organization that align with your values or identity. Your company may have employee resource groups that provide for a safe space to connect with others. Being around others who have a similar lived experience will provide a tremendous amount of support.

- If you can't find a community within your own organization, find an external organization that can provide support, resources and networking. Be around people who have the same lived experience and can have empathy for what you are going through. It makes all the difference.

- Write down all the things about yourself that you are proud of and read them back to yourself out loud. Remind yourself of your worth. Sometimes we forget.

MANAGER STRATEGIES

It is not enough to simply increase diversity hiring and tell people to bring their authentic selves to work. Without a culture of belonging, these good intentions will fail. Here are some ideas on how managers can support employees who bring their authentic selves to work.

Expect different opinions. If you hire a more diverse workforce, expect that you will get different opinions than you had before. Welcome these conversations rather than stifle or ask why they can't "just agree with everyone else." Instead, ask things like "Who has an idea that is *opposite* of what we have been discussing?" to make diverse perspectives the norm rather than the exception.

Pronouns matter. People use language and pronouns as a way to affirm their identity. As such, using the correct pronouns when referring to someone is very important. Use generic pronouns such as they/them before making any gender assumptions.

Give employees space to process emotions. Employees from underrepresented groups may have additional feelings of sadness, anger, frustration or stress that you may not experience. For example, if there is rising anti-Asian sentiment, expect that your Asian American employees are quietly suffering. Find ways to lighten work deliverables during these times and allow some time to process the tragedies of the day. Be conscious that these sorts of events may impact certain communities differently than they impact you.

Take responsibility for past missteps. We are all human and we are going to mess up. The important part is taking accountability when it happens. Instead of denying, defending or hoping it will blow over, acknowledge that you made a mistake, take responsibility for your actions and learn how you can do things differently. It starts by saying things like:

- "I am sorry. I made a mistake and didn't realize how this would impact you."

- "Will you help me? I want to get better."

- "Can you teach me? I am willing to learn."

9

The Power of Revealing Your Authentic Self

I REMEMBER HOW I felt the moment after I told my story to hundreds of my co-workers at Looker during National Hispanic Heritage Month. Moments before, my heart had been pounding and I was frightened about how people would react to my story. Unexpectedly, however, those nerves and anxieties were replaced with feelings of relief and gratitude. Relief that it was over. Gratitude that I had the courage to tell my story. Frankly, I had expected to feel that relief, but what I had not expected to feel was a newfound sense of purpose. As I was telling my story, I saw people's lives change before my eyes. I saw young Latinas in the audience seeing their future selves in me. I saw the CEO in the front row awakening to the real me. Sometimes I look back at that hour and I replay it in slow motion. It was as if something inside me had sparked.

I went home that evening and re-told the moment to Derek.

"My life changed today."

"What do you mean?"

"I think that this was the proudest moment in my life." Tears welled up in my eyes. "It was so hard to tell people my story, but when I finished, it was as if I was a new person."

I'm not sure why that moment was so transformative. I often wonder if I would have had the same feeling if it had fallen on deaf ears. If there had been silence, blank stares and no reaction. I don't know the answer to that question. I just know that sharing my personal story that afternoon changed me. I realized that storytelling was no longer just about me. It had a bigger purpose.

The words of Maya Angelou—"I come as one but stand as ten thousand"—made more sense to me now. Telling my story was no longer just about having the courage to stand up for me, it was about having the courage to stand up for everyone else like me who may not have the strength or privilege to do so. I realized that if I showed up and told my story, told the truth about the challenges I had faced, that it could change the lives of others.

Coming out of hiding is hard. There is a lot to unpack and potentially a lot to lose in the short term. But as we have seen over and over again with those who have let go of that burden, it is also freeing. It will not please everyone and some won't accept you, but over time you will realize that there is more support for you than you know. You will find that walking around in the world as who you are—truly are—is a breath of fresh air. And worth it.

Making the Decision to Finally Show Up as Your Authentic Self

Throughout this book we have followed the personal stories of Alexandra Navarro, Gena Cox, Jaleel Mackey and Tammy Ramos. At a certain point in their lives, each came to the same conclusion: that belonging begins with self-acceptance. Here are their individual stories of how they came to this realization.

ALEXANDRA NAVARRO'S STORY

Alexandra and her family had just moved to California. They decided to enroll their kids into a favorite local elementary school. When Alexandra showed up during the first week for the parent potluck, she realized right away that she was different. This school was Buddhist and most families were vegetarians. Alexandra was Colombian and loved meat. She slowly walked up to the potluck table, knowing that her spicy chicken wings were going to stand out like a sore thumb. That first night, she put those wings under the table and stayed quiet throughout the whole event. Once again, like in Florida and the Geo Metro incident, Alexandra felt out of place.

But Alexandra had been working on herself since the Geo Metro incident. She had gone on her year of self-discovery and had a better idea of how to handle this type of situation. After several months at her children's new school and trying to fit in to the new California organic lifestyle, Alexandra made a decision.

No more pretending.

This is me.

In Colombia we enjoy meat. Chicken wings is what I can offer to the world.

During the next potluck, instead of hiding the wings under the table, Alexandra proudly displayed them on the table next to the veggies and hummus. Families started trying this new cuisine and loved it. They told her, "Your wings are different and it's lovely. Thank you for sharing a part of you."

Putting out those chicken wings may seem like a small victory, but it's not. It's not about the chicken wings. It's about feeling 100-percent comfortable about sharing the real you with the rest of the world. It's about letting go of the need to fit in. The chicken wings were a small step, but an important one.

Alexandra kept showing up more and more as herself and, after a while, she realized that she was no longer pretending to be someone different. She got comfortable talking with people and worried less about her accent. When you ask Alexandra when she came to the realization that belonging begins with self-acceptance, she will tell you this:

I needed to believe in myself.

I needed to believe in Alexandra.

I needed to admire Alexandra.

I needed to respect Alexandra.

And that is when I started fitting in. When I really discovered who Alexandra was.

I now admire her, and respect her, and I am proud of her like she is my own child.

With this newfound sense of self, Alexandra's life has soared. She is now the chief of staff at a high-growth technology company and proudly showing up to work every day as exactly who she is.

DR. GENA COX'S STORY

I felt like the country cousin.

That is how Gena describes her experience during most of her professional career. She was like that distant cousin who shows up in the big city and doesn't know how to dress, talk or socially interact with the city folk. She simply didn't fit into corporate America. Even though she tried so desperately to play the part with her nicely tailored suits, she always knew that she was not totally "in" with her corporate surroundings.

After her personal awakening the night of the BET Awards, Gena realized that the first—and likely most important—thing she could do was to simply be more of Gena and less of this other fake person she had been for decades. She had to remove the uniform she had worn for so many years. Before that moment, if she was going to be on camera anywhere, for any reason, at any time, her hair was going to be laid, and she was going to be wearing a suit jacket. The reasons were simple—a desire to fit in, and the belief that if she put on the right clothes and had the right look, she would be accepted. So, she put on the uniform.

When I first met Gena, she was in the process of what she called "finding the real Gena." She and I had both joined the Top Three Book Workshop with AJ Harper, each of us determined to write a book that would transform lives. At the start of the workshop, she was what she termed "the fake Gena." Perfectly laid hair, a face full of make-up and a nicely tailored jacket. She spoke eloquently and with such ease. It wasn't until months later that I learned this was her famous facade. It was the same disguise she had worn every day for twenty years. During that three-month writing workshop, I got to witness the real Gena emerge.

Gena had faked it so well for so many years that it was all she knew. To become her true self, it was as if she had to find a new person. Her transformation started with small things, such as modifying her hours-long camera prep process. She ditched the straight hair, make-up and suits for no make-up, natural locs and T-shirts. She began filming short LinkedIn videos with her new look and noticed something positive right away. People loved the new, authentic Gena. New clients started to contact her. All of those fears she had made up in her mind about people not taking her seriously or trusting her advice if she didn't have the right corporate look disappeared. In fact, the complete opposite of what she expected happened. People began telling her to make more videos in her natural voice and appearance. When you ask Gena what she attributes this positive reaction to, she simply says, "I think it's because I look more relaxed, happier. Authentic. I look more like a real person."

Gena believes that being more herself has made her much more accessible to others. All that formality she was carrying around was a barrier to connection with others. It was pushing other people away. She was missing out on forming key relationships because people perceived her as too serious.

As she was reflecting on who the real Gena was, she asked herself, "Where is your sense of humor—where did it go?" She aspired to go back to the silly, spontaneous self she was back in high school and, as she put it, to go back to her original self. "That is such a weird thing to say," she thought.

JALEEL MACKEY'S STORY

When Jaleel returned to work after his stay at the trauma treatment facility, he was still too afraid to tell people what had happened to him, let alone about the domestic violence he had witnessed as a child or the suicidal thoughts that crossed his mind. He knew that rumors were swirling around the office as to why he had disappeared for three months but he did not want to answer any questions. He feared what his co-workers might think of him if they knew the truth. His company was fortunately very accommodating and provided him with a lower-stress job when he returned.

When the pandemic hit in 2020, he noticed something. People around him were struggling to make sense of it all, but he was surprised to find he was handling things pretty well. It wasn't because he knew all the answers, it was because he had acquired the right tools from his time at the treatment center to manage stress, anxiety and uncertainty. In particular, he learned how to process emotions. He understood that pain, sadness, anger, fear, guilt and shame are all part of our human experience, as is joy and passion. He now knew that you can't experience joy and passion until you make space for it. To illustrate his point, he shared with me this beautiful line from the poem *On Joy and Sorrow* by Kahlil Gibran: "The deeper that sorrow carves into your being, the more joy you can contain."

As he was transitioning back to a new normal, Jaleel realized that hiding all of his history, lived experiences and struggles with mental health was depriving others of a model that could show them they are not alone in their trauma or their battle with mental health. He understood that his life experiences were completely relevant and necessary in the world and that he had a responsibility to talk about them openly, especially as a man of color.

Jaleel decided he wanted to find a way to weave together these two identities: the high-performing, high-achieving professional Jaleel together with the healthy and grounded Jaleel. And he did just that. He joined a health-tech company whose mission is to destigmatize mental health care, break down barriers to access and give everyone the tools they need to proactively engage in their mental health. He intentionally sought out a new job that gave him the platform he needed to normalize these conversations. Jaleel's life mission is now to share his story willingly and freely so that people can see themselves in him and know there is a path to well-being even after they have endured trauma. More importantly, he wants to destigmatize mental health so people are unafraid to ask for help.

When I asked Jaleel what advice he would give to his younger self, he said this:

> It was all worth it. I wouldn't change any part of my story. If I had spiritually bypassed the crucible, I probably wouldn't be so grateful for the solid sense of well-being that I currently have. I feel fundamentally well because I know what fundamentally unwell feels like. That crucible of my life falling apart and me literally melting into Jaleel soup was so necessary for me in order to reconstruct my life from the ground up. My marriage is now beautiful. We know how

important it is to have our mental health foundation super strong. We prioritize ourselves and check in on each other regularly. I wouldn't change any bit of it.

TAMMY RAMOS'S STORY

Tammy's ex-husband would often make derogatory remarks about Mexicans around her. At the time, Tammy was pregnant with their first child and would just sit in silence as he made these comments. Finally, one day, it hurt her so much that she decided to call him out on it.

"What's the big deal?" her husband replied.

"Well... I'm Mexican. You know that," Tammy said.

"Oh, babe, I don't see you as Mexican, I see you like me."

Tammy couldn't believe what she had just heard. These words were extremely painful to hear because what her husband was saying to her was: "I don't love you as who you are, I love you only as I perceive you to be. You are good enough for me because I don't perceive you as Mexican."

It was the accumulation of these types of comments from friends, colleagues and family members over the years that finally led Tammy to make a change. Telling me this story, she remembered what she had said to herself:

Enough.

I won't be able to fit in everywhere, so I need to find where I fit in. As I am.

And not try to be somebody that I am not.

It is too painful to be around other people who don't accept me for who I am. So, let me find my people. Let me associate with those who embrace me as my true self.

As Tammy was evolving and learning to embrace her authentic self, she was invited back to her alma mater, St. Mary's College of California, to be a keynote speaker for their incoming students. The goal of the speech was to inspire students of color to pursue their dreams and to serve as a role model: if Tammy could do it, so could they.

In preparing for her speech, Tammy came to a realization. She no longer wanted to pretend. These kids deserved better. So, that day, she decided to take off her mask and tell her real story, all of it, including about her unwed teenage mom, her Mexican roots, the orphanage and her humble beginnings. She didn't go into the speech with any expectations, but what happened next surprised her. She received a huge outpouring of love and support from the students, faculty and administration. Everyone sitting in that auditorium that day felt inspired and encouraged by Tammy's story. That was the beginning of her recognizing that part of her destiny is sharing her story so that it can encourage and inspire others to know that *sí se puede*. It doesn't matter where you come from, or what you look like, or what your gender is. There is nothing you cannot accomplish with focus, hard work and faith.

Today, Tammy proudly tells her story. She emphasizes that it is not always easy to be one's authentic self. It may not be for everyone. However, she has learned that, if you are rejected by someone, it is not rejection of you as a person. It is a reflection of them, not you. She no longer allows those rejections to define her. Tammy attributes much of her self-confidence and success to her faith. If she could speak to little girl Tammy, who felt lost, insecure, sad, lonely and fearful of the future, she would say: "Always be looking for what your purpose is. What have you been called to do in this world? Life will have twists and turns as you move from one season to the next. Stay focused, work hard and cling to your faith. Your destiny is already in progress."

Revealing Your Authentic Self May Take Some Time

Hiding serves its purpose. It allows you to move through the world with less friction. It feels easier to be like everyone else and not stand out. But is that true? Is there really less friction? I would argue that friction was always there, it was just that you decided that making *yourself* uncomfortable was better than making someone else uncomfortable. While this may allow you to achieve your short-term goals (promotion, friendships, whatever they may be), it will not allow you to meet your long-term goal of acceptance and a sense of belonging.

For some, making the decision to show up as their authentic self can happen in a split second, and for others it can take weeks, months or even years. When you have spent so much time and energy hiding something about yourself from the rest of the world, the decision to show up authentically is frightening.

All of the self-doubt and fears start whirling around in your mind:

What if people don't accept me?

What if I lose the credibility I have worked so hard to earn?

What if I start getting treated differently?

What if people start looking down at me?

The "what-ifs" start piling up and it seems like the risk is too high. But, eventually, at some point, the weight and burden of hiding becomes too large to carry, and these risks, while seemingly large, become worth taking. If you have followed the steps in this book, you will have begun to assemble the tools you need to take this step. You have started to build your community of people (or you are at least thinking about who might be on that list); you are practicing self-care, combating perfectionism, and looking for a sponsor or mentor to support you. With these people and newly acquired skills, you are ready to take the next step. You are ready because you now realize you have the strength to overcome any potential setbacks.

As you have read throughout this book, you have seen many moments in my life when my true self was not enough. Unpacking all of those moments took time. It was not easy or without confusion, frustration and pain. I realized that, for me, it was a slow awakening that came over time and, frankly, is still unfolding. For Alexandra, Gena, Jaleel and Tammy, the experience was similar. While there may have been a moment that stood out in their mind as the day they decided to make a change, it was the years of discomfort before that moment that led to that decision.

That exact moment to reveal your authentic self may not be crystal clear at first. It may occur slowly. You can start by revealing one small thing at a time. With each small reveal, you will start noticing that you have more support than you realized. You will also start feeling that overwhelming sense of relief of not having to pretend anymore. With each small reveal, the burden will feel less and less.

Revealing Can Start with the Little Things

It's interesting how a physical attribute like your hairstyle can be so meaningful. Gena chose to straighten her hair rather than wear her natural locs. I did the same for most of my career. If I don't blow-dry my hair, I get a million curls and lots of frizz. My friends would often tell me how lucky I was for having natural curls. But I didn't feel lucky. I am not sure where along the way I internalized the belief that curly, frizzy hair is not "professional" and that straight hair would make me less Latino and more acceptable, but shortly after I started my career, I began straightening my hair. I continued straightening it throughout my legal career and even as I was juggling two small children at home—I would spend hours each morning drying and then flat-ironing my hair to make it perfectly straight.

After I left my corporate job and during my "year of transformation," I remembered that my hair stylist had once told me it isn't good to dry your hair every day. Since I no longer had to go into the office and wasn't seeing clients every day, I decided to let it air dry. I didn't have much to lose. If it looked weird, nobody would see it. So, I got rid of the blow dryer and flat iron.

At first, it felt odd. I didn't like it and I thought others wouldn't like how I looked.

But then something unexpected happened. People liked my natural hair. I even felt more relaxed and myself with my natural hair. I also got an extra hour back in my day. Instead of spending that time getting my hair "perfectly straight," I spent it exercising or catching up on sleep. I kept my hair natural for years, even after I started my new job at Looker. I remember thinking twice before I went to that job interview about whether or not I should straighten my hair, but, ultimately, I chose to leave my natural curls in place.

Still, whenever it was time to take a corporate headshot or do a press interview, I reverted back to my old habit of straightening my hair. My theory that straight hair was somehow more professional or would garner more respect was so deeply engrained in me that I didn't realize I still held that belief until years later.

It's Easy to Revert Back to Hiding

After I left Looker, I decided that I wanted to seek out a corporate board seat. At this point in my life, I felt much more confident in who I was. I had started a DEI program from the ground up and was mentoring other start-ups on how to build theirs. I had put the whole hiding piece behind me. I put together a board bio and mastered my board pitch, and then it was time to update my professional headshot. I scheduled an appointment with a local photographer for a Monday morning. I flawlessly planned every detail leading up to the session (as a perfectionist would). I scheduled a haircut on Friday, and asked the stylist to do a blowout. My plan was to keep that beautiful straight blowout in place until Monday morning. However, on Friday afternoon, in the middle of my haircut, I got a call from my daughter telling me that I had pick her up early. We had miscommunicated the pick-up time, and so I had to leave before the blowout was done. I begged my stylist to try to squeeze me in over the weekend and she agreed. So, grabbing my purse, I hurried out of the salon with my hair dripping wet. It air-dried as I drove to pick up my daughter.

All of those bouncy curls showed up just as I expected them to. What I didn't anticipate was the reaction later that evening. We had some friends over and they commented on how much they loved my curls. Even my teenage daughters, who normally frown at all my fashion choices, told me how much they loved my wavy hair. I kept receiving compliments all weekend long but, despite these accolades, later that night during our family dinner I mentioned to my daughters that I was going to straighten my hair the next day in anticipation of my photo shoot on Monday.

"What?" they asked, surprised. "Mom, you should leave your hair exactly the way it is."

"I was planning on using the headshots for my board search so I want them to look professional. Curly hair is not professional."

Both of my daughters, at the time seventeen and fourteen, tilted their heads. My oldest daughter Sophia looked me directly in the eyes and said, "Mom. We've sat here all year long listening to you tell people about being their authentic selves. You have to be your authentic self, too. Your curly hair is you, not the straight hair."

I stared back at them in silence. Feeling a little annoyed, to be honest. Have you heard the saying that your children are your best teachers? In that moment, they were my best teachers. My girls had spent the last year overhearing me encourage countless women and girls to show up as their true self as I mentored them on Zoom, and here I was about to do the exact opposite. They repeated my advice right back to me. I hadn't even realized I was reverting back to my old ways.

When Hiding Is No Longer Just About You

That day with my teenage daughters was another pivotal moment for me. *They were watching me.* I realized that this simple decision about how I would style my hair was suddenly a life lesson. If I made the choice to hide once again, it would no longer simply impact me, it would impact their view of the world, too. This was bigger than just me. This was about how I wanted my daughters to show up in the world.

I looked at my daughters, confused. I thought: *Yes, they are watching me. But board work is totally different. I know what that boardroom looks like and it usually doesn't include someone who looks like me. I need to make it easy for board members to accept me, not add another obstacle.*

On the one hand, I didn't want to lose out on getting a board seat by trying to prove a point about authenticity for my kids. I was frightened to show up being "too big" or "too Latina" with my curly dark hair and strong personality. But I knew in my gut that my daughters were right. I could no longer hide and be someone I was not.

For me, my authentic self was my vibrant curly hair. If I was going to ask people to show up authentically in the world, how could I not do it myself? I wish I could tell you that it was an easy decision once I became aware of it, but it was not. Some of you may think, "What is the big deal about your hair?" It may seem like a superficial thing and something that doesn't matter, but for me it was not about fashion. It was about worthiness. The style I chose represented whether or not I thought I was good enough. The decades of indoctrination of what I was "supposed to look like" at work were so deep in me that I could not let it go.

My daughters were watching me.

After many hours of consideration, I finally texted my stylist and canceled the appointment. I decided to take the headshots with my curly hair, but let me tell you—I was really nervous about that decision.

The next day, midway through the photo shoot, the photographer asked whether I wanted to glance at a couple of the pictures on his camera to make sure I was happy with them. Nervously, I said yes. I walked over to his camera and looked down at the images. Slowly, a huge smile came across my face. My kids were right. I absolutely loved the pictures. Not because I looked great, but because I looked like me.

SELF-REFLECTION MOMENT

- Think back to the self-reflection exercise in Chapter 8. Now, list the one thing about yourself that you have not revealed to others. Why are you hiding that particular thing? What fear comes up for you at the thought of revealing it?

- If you feel you ready, consider beginning to slowly reveal what you've been hiding. For example, if you've been hiding behind the wrong gender identity, add your pronouns to your signature line. If you've been hiding behind your hairstyle, wear your natural locs on Zoom. If you've been hiding an invisible disability, mention it casually in a conversation. Whatever the thing is that you have kept quiet all these years and feel a sense of shame around, try revealing it slowly to someone you trust or in a setting that feels safe. You could even reveal it to a total stranger in a way that will have no consequences. Just say it or do it out loud and see how that feels.

- After the first time you reveal what you have been hiding, notice your emotions. How did it feel to say out loud the thing that you have never said out loud before? Notice how your body feels. Is there a sense of relief? Is their fear? Do you think you could maybe do it again? Remember: small steps, repeated often.

Your Difference Adds Value

While I wrote this book in part to support others who struggle with showing up as their authentic self, there was also another reason. We need your authentic self in the room. Not the phony self that goes along with the crowd, but the real you.

Having worked with executives and sat in boardrooms for over twenty-five years, I can tell you that there is still one single perspective dominating most decision-making. As statistics tell us, most board and C-suite members are white heterosexual males with very similar lived experiences. Yes, we need those perspectives too, and, yes, we need people with decades of experience at the table, but I believe we also need other viewpoints. Our workforce is changing. The next generation is looking to work differently. Consumer profiles and demographics are more diverse. Without different opinions at the table, companies will not see their blind spots. Our organizations need your different perspective to help them succeed. Your difference adds value. You see things from a unique lens.

While I was at Looker, the company decided to sell to Google. In many ways it was bittersweet. It was a phenomenal exit—the company was valued at $2.6 billion—so it was a great result for the company's shareholders and employees, but we had all fallen in love with the culture at Looker and many of us were not ready to let it go.

As we were preparing for the transition to Google, COVID-19 hit. It was March 2020 and Google had told us they were going to shut down the offices. As offices started to close and schools were shutting down, we were all collectively coming to grips with the understanding that COVID-19 was not going to be just a two-week break.

I realized within a few weeks of the shutdown that this was going to be hard on our employees. And since I once had little ones at home and I had been through the struggle of balancing young kids and a demanding job, I also knew this was going to be particularly hard on working parents.

We were coming to the end of the quarter, which is usually crunch time. We were holding one of our weekly staff meetings and going through the normal agenda: deals in the pipeline, deals closed, deals pushed and so on. The team was focused on the numbers even though we were all living in this new strange Zoom reality. As I sat there listening to the conversation, I realized that nobody was talking about the employees.

How are they doing?

How is working from home working for them?

Do they need support?

Is anyone at their breaking point?

I had been talking with the various leaders of the ERGs at Looker during this time and I knew things were not going well for most of our people. I had spent hours checking in with members of my legal team and I could hear the despair in their voices. As a parent and a DEI leader, I knew that there was a lot going on with our employees and that we needed to be talking about it at the executive level. As I thought about how long COVID-19 might last, I knew intuitively that if we did not focus our attention on the well-being of our employees—whether they were parents, single people struggling with isolation or anyone suffering through any one of many individual battles we all went through during that time—they would not make it. Burnout is real. The struggle to keep it all together is too hard, and was being made exponentially harder by the pandemic. At the end of the revenue discussion, I knew I had to share my concerns.

I offered my feedback about what I was seeing with my own group and with the employees in the ERGs. I explained how difficult asking our employees to switch to remote working in an instant had been for them. As I shared my perspective, other executives chimed in about what they were seeing in their own groups—an echo of vocal support that was so critical in galvanizing us all to take action. From there, a great discussion began and we started talking about things we could do to take care of our employees. I often think of that moment, because it demonstrates the importance of having a diverse perspective in the room. While making the numbers is, of course, a priority, I had the ability to see things from a different lens. As a management team, we had to figure out how to keep the business running while at the same time supporting our employees. Without the latter, we could not succeed in the former. In that executive meeting, my lived experiences mattered. My difference added value and I had the courage to speak up.

Having a diverse board can also make a difference, and I have seen this first-hand. Lynn Vojvodich was the only female board director at Looker. She was actually only one of three women that I had ever seen on a board of directors at an enterprise software company during my twenty-five-year career. I was excited to see a women join the board, but what I didn't realize was how much of a difference her simple presence would make.

We were holding one of our regular board meetings and going through the business-as-usual sales report, financial results, product updates. It was the time of year when we also approved the company's annual bonus plan and executive compensation.

As we were going through the materials, Lynn casually asked, "Have we ever done a gender wage gap analysis?"

"No," our CEO replied.

"Maybe we can add that to the agenda for next year. It would be great to see how we are doing on that front," said Lynn.

And that was it. With one simple question, we were off conducting a gender wage gap analysis. It was something that we knew we needed to do, but always seemed to fall off the priority list. In all my years sitting in the boardroom, I had never heard a board member ask about whether we were paying our employees equally. It was not coincidence that this question came from our sole female board member. Lynn did not ask the question to make a point or raise a fuss. She just had a different perspective.

Any woman who has risen to the executive ranks of an enterprise software company knows that a gender wage gap exists. Most companies are not intentionally paying women less. Research shows that women tend to not negotiate their salaries or seek promotions as compared to their male counterparts and, as a result, companies unwittingly pay women less for the same work. The gap creeps in over time. Lynn's presence in the boardroom that day and the question she asked made a difference.

NEXT SMALL THING
It is time to tell your story (or even part of your story). To anybody. It does not have to be to a room full of people. You can start with a close friend. Your pastor or rabbi. The mail carrier. Just say it out loud and see how it feels.

One Story Can Change the World

In writing this book I am telling you my story. In telling her story at St. Mary's College, Tammy Ramos is making a difference to first-generation students. Telling your story can change the world, because someone who hears it who thought she was the only one feeling unseen, unappreciated or unworthy will realize she is not alone. It is especially impactful to hear that someone you admire and who you thought always "had it together" has felt the same way as you. If you are a person who still in hiding, this knowledge can give you the confidence that you too can make this transformation. That is how I felt when

I heard Abby Wambach's story on the *We Can Do Hard Things* podcast with her wife, Glennon Doyle. Abby Wambach is one of the most decorated athletes in the United States. She is a two-time Olympian, a FIFA Women's World Cup champion, a six-time winner of the U.S. Soccer Player of the Year award, the highest all-time goal scorer as a forward for the national team and, with 184 goals, second in international goals for both female and male soccer players.

In an episode called "Being Brave," Abby recalls the moment when she decided to take off her mask. She was in Germany for the 2011 World Cup and they were about to play a critical game. Instead of squeezing in some more practices, Abby decided to get her hair cut. Not an ordinary haircut. Instead, Abby decided that she needed to cut off her ponytail. This may not seem like a big deal for some people, but for Abby it was much more than a haircut. This ponytail symbolized everything she was not. The ponytail was the look that female athletes were supposed to wear. She knew that to get the attention of sponsors and be part of the elite female soccer world, she had to look the part: feminine and "straight-passing." After many years of hiding her sexual orientation from the world, in that hair salon, alone in Germany, she decided it was time to reveal who she really was. She wanted her "outsides to match her insides," as she says. So, she cut that ponytail off and transformed her look into the iconic Abby Wambach cut that is now worn by millions of kids across the world.

Her immediate reaction after she cut her hair was fear. Fear that she would not be accepted. Fear that she would lose endorsements. Fear that she would not belong. That fear quickly lifted when she returned to her team. They whole-heartedly embraced her, and her life took a different turn that day.

Following this transformative haircut, Abby went on to have one of the most memorable goals in soccer history. In the 122nd minute of the World Cup quarterfinal match against Brazil, she scored the equalizer in stoppage time, helping the Americans later progress to the championship final game against Japan. Her last-minute goal set a new record for latest goal ever scored in a match and was awarded with ESPN's 2011 ESPY Award for best play of the year.

As Abby recalls that historic header, she attributes her ability to elevate to new levels directly to that simple haircut. She no longer had to carry the weight of showing up as someone else on that soccer field. Without that burden of pretending to be something she was not, Abby could walk into a higher, bigger, more purposeful version of her life. On the podcast, Abby says, "Sometimes when we allow our inner selves to match our outer selves everything becomes aligned." That day in Germany, her outer self finally matched her inner self. And by her telling her story, she made countless of others feel seen. By me telling my story, I hope to do the same.

Tell your story.

It can make a difference.

MANAGER STRATEGIES

The day has come and your employee has decided to show up more authentically at work! Now, your job as their manager is to accept and support. Here are some tips for that moment.

Initiate courageous conversations. Don't be afraid to ask questions. Once, a manager told me how he had misinterpreted an employee's behavior during a meeting. The employee, who was from Asia, was looking at the floor while the manager was speaking to her. He took her behavior as not caring, but the opposite was true. She was showing respect for his seniority in a way that is customary in Asia. Instead of making assumptions based on your own life experiences, be open and curious and ask questions about cultural norms. Be willing to have a courageous conversation about things you may not understand.

Step back. The greatest gift you can give someone who feels invisible is the opportunity to be seen. Resist the urge to speak for them, dominate the conversation or explain an idea on their behalf. Instead, pass the mic, give them proper attribution and don't take credit for work they did. By simply stepping back and giving them the stage, you are signaling that you value what they bring to the table.

Be kind. I can't tell you how many times people from underrepresented groups have told me that the one thing they wish people would do is simply be kind. That's it. Before you make jokes or comments, pause and consider whether your remarks are potentially harmful to a specific group or identity. You have no idea what is happening in someone's personal life and your words or jokes could be devastating. This is especially true for someone who is trying to muster up the courage to be vulnerable and reveal their whole self at work but finds themselves in an environment that doesn't value or respect their identity.

10

You Are a Role Model

I WATCHED *AMERICAN IDOL* for over a decade. For anyone who isn't familiar with this show, it is a singing competition that looks for the next superstar. It has in fact produced several celebrities over the years, including Kelly Clarkson and Carrie Underwood. While the singing is great, the part I enjoy most is hearing the stories of each contestant. A wide variety of artists try out for this competition. The cowboy, the pop artist, the R&B singer, the coffeehouse guitarist—each with their own unique style.

Over the years, the most fascinating part has been watching the contrast between a contestant who shows up as their real self no matter how messy or awkward they may be versus someone who shows up looking and acting the role perfectly in an attempt to be what they think the judges are looking for.

As each person competes, it becomes very apparent who is genuine and who is putting on an act. As audience members, we pick up on authenticity instantly. There is a notable difference between the singer-songwriter who shows up with his worn-out boots and a hat weathered from being out on the farm all day and sings his own handwritten song in a southern drawl and the suburban teen who shows up with his shiny silver belt buckle and a brand-new cowboy hat to sing a well-known Garth Brooks song. Both want to get the coveted "cowboy" slot on the show. Both are singing country songs and are likely great singers. But only one is making a connection with us. It quickly becomes clear that wearing the clothes and acting the part is not enough. We instantly connect with the young man who grew up on the farm and shows up a little weathered, but himself. But why don't we apply this same lesson from *American Idol* to our own lives? Why must we think we have to wear the right clothes, say the right things and act the part to belong?

Like *American Idol* stars, we know authenticity when we see it. We see it in the people who show up as themselves, unapologetically. They are not worried about how they may be judged or what others may say about them. They are usually less than perfect, but they are authentic. If you are like me, these are the type of people that you are interested in knowing.

You Can Impact Others by Simply Being You

Cornell Verdeja-Woodson has held numerous DEI positions in both high tech and academia, including at companies such as Headspace, Google, Looker and Cornell University. He has his bachelor of science from Ithaca College and his master's degree from the University of Vermont and he is working on his doctoral degree at USC. He and I worked together at Looker in building its first-ever DEI program. Not only did I learn DEI fundamentals from Cornell, more importantly, I learned about the value of authenticity from simply watching him.

My advice to my younger self would have been to start as early as possible showing up as my authentic self. Even as early as high school.

That is what Cornell told me one day as we were talking about the value of bringing our authentic selves to work. He explained the exact moment when he learned this. He was in the middle of his master's program and was interviewing for an assistantship position. Cornell walked into the interview as he always does: confident, funny and transparent. Not trying to prove anything or be anyone different than exactly who he is. After the interview, the gentleman who would have been his boss told him what an impact that made:

"Wow. You just empowered me so much to do that myself."

"Do what?"

"Do that. What you just did. You just said it. Like nothing."

What had struck this person was Cornell referring to himself as a gay Black man. The interviewer was an older gentleman who had spent his entire career in the traditional halls of universities and had not had the luxury of showing up as a gay Black man during those days.

He told Cornell, "I never felt safe to do that. But now you just gave me the courage to show up as a gay Black man."

Wow! was all Cornell could think to himself.

Cornell did not realize he could make such an impact by simply being unabashedly himself. By moving through life with no pretense, Cornell had changed this person's life.

Don't underestimate the impact you can have by simply sharing who you are and how you see the world. You never know who is in the room and who may be watching. By just being yourself, you may be giving someone else the courage to do the same thing.

The Ripple Effect of Role Modeling Authenticity

In my research for this book, I interviewed two top female executives and board members, who each shared with me similar epiphanies as Cornell had. Elena Donio, who you first met in Chapter 3, and Lynn Vojvodich, who I introduced to you in the last chapter, are at the top of their industries, and each has had the experience of realizing the value that showing up authentically can have on others.

ELENA DONIO'S STORY

Elena is a C-suite executive, board member and investor. But when you ask her what it felt like to be a young woman in tech at the beginning of her career, she will tell you that it was lonely. Elena usually found herself around tables of men. She started her career at the well-known consulting firm Accenture and after several years moved over to Deloitte Consulting as a senior manager. At Deloitte, there were very few women leaders and those that were in positions of decision-making capability were living very different lives than what she envisioned for herself. They were fantastic female leaders with brilliant business minds, but likely had made some tough choices along the way to reach the top of their profession. Elena dreamed of something different for herself. She wanted to rise to the top, but she also wanted to get married, have a family and not spend most of her days on the road. The women that she saw around her during those early consulting days did not exemplify what she wanted for her life.

As she progressed through her career, Elena was in constant search of the right balance. How do you sit in places of authority, in positions where you can make the decisions that impact people's lives and the direction of technologies, but at the same time have a partner, a family, hobbies and a meaningful life? She desperately wanted to take a seat at the table but did not want to lose herself in the process. She kept looking for that one female leader who could show her how it could be done… but she never saw one.

After several years in the consulting world, Elena joined a start-up that was quickly acquired by Concur, a travel and expense software company, where she had an amazing eighteen-year career that ultimately landed her as president. Elena was surrounded by some wonderful men during her time at Concur. Men who lifted her up in incredible ways. From them, she learned how to show up at work and how to be an executive. This was a group of men who were brilliant at what they did and were amazing business thinkers and leaders, but they also gave enormous amounts of themselves to the company and its growth in ways that she found very hard to replicate. It was extremely difficult to keep up with the air miles and the time they put in the office. She tried the best she could to duplicate that style of work, but in doing so she lost a little bit of who she was, and sacrificed many things. She justified those sacrifices because she believed it was what was required to compete—not necessarily against her colleagues but with the industry as a whole.

Elena eventually hit a wall when her two boys were at the ages of about three-and-a-half and eighteen months. She realized that she wasn't doing anything particularly well anymore, at least not to her own expectations. She decided to tell her then-boss that it was time to leave.

"I'm going to leave. I need to take some time. I don't know that I can do this," she told her boss, who was the founder and COO of Concur.

He stared at Elena. He knew how valuable she was to the company, and knew he had to keep her there.

"What about working part-time? Or what about a different role?" He kept proposing different solutions. What about this. What about that.

As Elena thought about the various scenarios, she realized she had no idea how to show up in a new way at work. She had never seen it done.

I don't know how to do part-time.

I don't know how to do it differently.

I don't know how to not to be fully engaged.

She only knew one speed. In her mind, it was a zero-sum game. Either she showed up full-time as a leader with little time for family and friends, or she had to duck out entirely. So, she decided to duck out.

Elena spent one year at home, finding a new balance as a parent and committing herself to making up for lost time. But during this period she also missed being in the action. What Elena didn't realize is that she had just gone through her period of contraction and was ready for her expansion phase.

Around the same time, her former boss at Concur offered her a new position. As she was considering it, she came up with the litany of things she needed to put in place in order for her to go back to work: less traveling, preserving family dinner time, a flexible schedule, and so on. She decided to meet with the COO to tell him about her lengthy list of requirements. One by one she listed them off, feeling proud of the boundaries she was setting for herself. He listened to the whole list. When she finished, he paused and then smiled at her.

"You know you are talking to yourself right now, not me, right? I would take 50 percent of you if that is all I can have. Because 50 percent of you is as good as 100 percent of most people."

Elena was speechless. Someone believing in her like that was exactly what she needed in that moment. She returned to Concur and started showing up differently. She went home at scheduled times, reduced her travel schedule, attended family and friend's events. But while she had more of a work/life balance, when she showed up at work, she switched into work mode and didn't speak much about her family.

It wasn't until a number of years later that a well-loved colleague—single, male, and gay—made her question everything, again. When he decided to start a family, alone, she watched in awe at how he parented his twin babies.

Like he did everything else, he parented *loudly.*

"We have a double ear infection; what do I do?"

"I haven't slept in four days. How do you do it?"

"I am up to my elbows in baby poop! Just had a triple blow out. When does this stop?"

He would talk about the twins during meetings, in the halls, on the phone, and even on stage. The twins were a part of him and his life, and it was apparent everywhere he went. Everyone at work knew about the twins, had seen their pictures and heard their stories. Soon, by simply watching a different style of showing up, Elena realized that she was doing it all wrong. Here were these two kids that everybody in the office knew better than her own two boys who had been around a heck of a lot longer. But nobody knew about Elena's kids because Elena never brought that part of herself to work as fully or completely as her colleague did. Her family life stayed at home because she had never seen it done any other way.

Elena realized that, by keeping her kids and parenting struggles firmly separate from her professional identity, she was not only letting herself down, she was, more importantly, letting everyone around her down, especially the next generation of talent. Right in front of her was this thing that she had so desperately wanted to see as a young female executive and she wasn't doing it herself. Her younger self would have died to see another woman having a family proudly and leading a company all at the same time. A younger Elena had been looking for validation that it was not only normal to work and have a family, but that it was *worth* doing.

It was in that moment that Elena decided she had to show up differently in the workplace. She decided that she had to be more open and transparent about life, its struggle, its beauty and its dimensionality. She came to believe that if we show up at work as our true full selves, that is ultimately how we get our best work done.

As a result of showing up authentically at work, Elena not only became a more relatable leader, she became a more fully expressed person. She ended up having a third child and it was no accident that everybody at work knew everything about this new addition to the family.

LYNN VOJVODICH'S STORY

Lynn is an accomplished board member, investor and former chief marketing officer at Salesforce. She graduated from Stanford with a bachelor of science in product design and received an MBA from Harvard. She started her career as a structural design engineer in very male-dominated industries, such as designing offshore oil structures and working on aerospace and construction projects. She was literally the only female engineer among thousands, so she had to figure out how to fit into these environments. She would wear button-up suits and she rarely showed emotion at work. She wanted to earn the respect of the men around her and believed—perhaps rightfully so at the time—that she had to downplay being a woman.

Things changed for Lynn when she joined BEA Systems and started working for a man who was running the marketing function at the company. This person led differently. Lynn was accustomed to a conservative, "no joking around" type of environment. But her new boss was different. He was funny and goofy and brought his whole self to work. He would talk about his family and all the craziness of parenting young kids. Watching him lead in this manner opened Lynn up to bringing more of her own self to work. Soon, she started having more empathy and realized that everyone is dealing with hard things at home that we don't see. This became especially true after she had kids. With the sleepless nights and endless worries, she now understood the difficulties of balancing work and kids.

A decade later, Lynn was sitting on the board of directors at Ford. She had a board meeting coming up but was nursing her daughter at the time. She decided she needed to tell the board chair and the CEO that she needed to take a break every few hours to pump. She knew she needed to do this not only for herself, but for all working women. So, she told them what was going to happen, and she did it in a matter-of-fact way. No apologies.

Hearing Lynn's story was particularly impactful for me. I wish I had seen someone like her when I first had my kids. Then, maybe, I would have had the courage to ask for a break to either pump or breastfeed my daughter during an eight-hour board meeting.

I remember one board meeting very well. As was typical, we held our committee meetings on the same day as the board meeting, so the day was long. I was corporate secretary of the company, so I had to attend every meeting and take the minutes. We usually had a short lunch break and that was when I was planning to pump.

I had recently come back from maternity leave. I was nursing my daughter every two to three hours. As I described earlier in this book, I would normally either go home to nurse or my husband would bring my daughter to the parking garage so that I could nurse her quickly in between meetings. Once she got on the bottle, I was able to pump at work.

I had tried to pump as much as I could immediately prior to the morning meeting. I was planning to pump again during our lunch break, but our committee meetings had run long and the board had decided we would have a working lunch then go straight into the next meeting without a break. We could eat while management made their presentations.

I sat frozen.

We had started at 8 a.m.

218 EMBRACE THE POWER OF YOU

It was now noon.

We would have no break.

Meetings were to end at 4 p.m.

Calculating quickly in my head, I realized that this schedule would mean I would not relieve my poor breasts for almost eight hours. Could I go that long? How much will it hurt? Will I start leaking in the middle of the meeting? I desperately wanted to ask someone if we could take a quick fifteen-minute break so I could pump, but I was literally the only woman in the boardroom, and the youngest person there as well. I felt completely intimidated by this room full of older white men. I decided it was too risky and frankly too embarrassing to say something. So, I grabbed my lunch, brought it back to the table with the others and continued.

The time slowly crept on and with every hour my breasts got fuller and fuller with milk. It was like a cruel physical reminder my body was giving me to tell me that I was not at home nursing my little girl. As we started getting closer to 4 p.m., my breasts could not take it anymore, and they started leaking. We were in the middle of a serious conversation about budgets and strategy, so I could not disappear without providing an explanation. But neither did I have the courage to explain what was going on. So, I sat, hoping and praying that the meeting would end soon and that the leaking would be minimal. I was wearing nursing pads but I could still feel milk leaking through to my blouse. Luckily, I was wearing a suit jacket that day—so I casually buttoned it up. I didn't even look down to check if there were any wet stains. Part of me didn't want to know.

The meeting finally finished. I ran to my office and grabbed the breast pump to relieve myself.

I think back on that day and imagine how different it could have been for me if there had been a board member like Lynn there, someone who had once spoken up to ask for breaks so she could nurse her baby or pump. If she were sitting in that boardroom, I know I would have asked for her advice on how to manage this eight-hour board meeting. Or, what if the CEO had been female—someone who had also returned from maternity leave and often took breaks to pump or nurse? Or, what if there were a male CEO who was like Lynn's boss and often talked about his kids and the struggles of parenting? Or, what if there were a Moms ERG or a Parents ERG where I could have asked for tips? None of that existed for me. So, I sat there and managed the situation alone. In silence. Frustrated, scared, embarrassed and lonely.

Bringing your whole self to work not only benefits you, it benefits those around you. The young mom who is scared to ask for pumping breaks. The gay man who is nervous to talk about his husband. The parent who misses his children's sports activities to make a good impression. If they all saw someone like themselves fully expressing themselves at work, they would be more likely to be themselves as well.

Correct People When They Make Assumptions About You

As I've shared, people have made incorrect assumptions about me many times. Some have assumed I was white. Others have assumed I was the paralegal. On the playground, I am assumed to be the stay-at-home mom (or even the stereotypical Hispanic nanny) and not the breadwinner. Until recently, I stayed quiet when people made these mistakes about me. I was too embarrassed, or I didn't feel like trying to correct them, or I simply didn't have the energy. But my perspective on that changed during a recent video call.

I was on the call with several participants. The facilitator asked us each to introduce ourselves and give our pronouns:

he/him, she/her or they/them. We went around, and one of the participants—a presenting leader in the call—shared that their pronouns were "they/them." This was a little surprising to some of us, because this person had presented as female in previous events and we were accustomed to referring to them as "she/her." I made a mental note of it so I would refer to them properly in the future. Later in the call, while they were leading a discussion, another participant asked a question and unfortunately addressed them with the wrong pronouns. I noticed it right away and got nervous for this person. But instead of continuing the conversation or letting it slide like I probably would have, they interrupted and corrected him.

"I just wanted to remind you that I go by the pronouns they or them."

Everyone in the call got quiet and all eyes were on the person that had used the wrong pronouns. He gracefully apologized and made an earnest effort to use the right pronouns going forward.

In that moment, I realized how important it was for that leader to make this correction. By calling out the mistake, they brought awareness about how much this mattered not only to the person who made the error but also to the rest of us. They were intentionally trying to disrupt the culture of making assumptions based on gender expression and we needed to respect that. I smiled and was so impressed with this person's courage.

It reminded me that this is still a muscle I need to exercise. I have stayed quiet and in the background for so many years that correcting people's assumptions of me is still not easy and certainly not second nature.

NEXT SMALL THING

Notice the next time someone makes an incorrect assumption about you. If you feel like it is a safe environment, try to correct it. It doesn't have to be a big fanfare—simply correct it and move on. How does it feel to correct people? How did people react? This is truly a muscle and you will notice over time that this will get easier to do.

You May Not Always Be Able to Show Up Authentically

Even if you are confident in who you are, you may not always be able to show up authentically in every situation. While Cornell never kept his identity a secret, early in his career he often kept his feelings around certain social issues hidden. Everybody knew he was Black, that he was gay, and that he grew up poor, but he kept his feelings around racism, homophobia and how these things show up in the workplace to himself out of fear of being "the angry Black man" or "the angry gay man" He learned that he needed to become palatable to people to be liked or get promoted.

But, as he grew in his career, he came to learn that even hiding your thoughts on an issue is not showing up authentically. Embracing your whole self means not only embracing your race, gender or sexual identity, it also means not being afraid to bring your diverse perspective or challenging thoughts to the workplace. Cornell is no longer afraid to speak up, but he does carefully pick and choose when to use his energy. He is aware that there could be repercussions for giving his perspective. He has learned that he needs to actively protect his own mental health and emotional well-being, so there are moments when he decides to simply let things go, when he decides that this is not where he wants to use his social capital to make change. If you go after everything, he explained to me, you will be exhausted. So, he intentionally challenges those things that are most important to him and that have the most impact.

The other factor relevant to whether you can express your authenticity freely at work is privilege. Earlier in my career, when I was a young attorney in a sea of older white men, I did not have the privilege of being different or having a contrarian view. I was the sole breadwinner at home and had a lot to lose financially and professionally. Later in my career, when I had built a community of support and some financial freedom, I had the ability to be more of myself. Each of us has to assess our situation to see what potential repercussions there might be for challenging the status quo. For some, these repercussions may be worth it. For others, they may not. And for yet others, they may be worth it, but only at certain times. For Cornell, at this point in his life, if he has something important to say, he will say it. Even if he has something to lose. He says it because it is so important. He says it not for himself but to give voice to those who are voiceless.

Create Space for People to Show Up Authentically

When I first met Cornell, he shared with me that he had started off his career as a wedding planner.

"A wedding planner? That must have been hard!" I replied.

"Yes," he said. "If you can manage to keep a wedding couple happy, you can do anything!"

Cornell explained that his DEI work was beginning even in his role as a wedding planner. When talking with brides, his first question would always be: "Tell me about your guests."

The brides would ask him why he was asking about that and why it mattered.

"It matters because when we are picking a venue, I want to make sure that we are picking a place that meets the needs of *all* your guests. I want to make sure that any guests with disabilities, or mobility issues, or whose eyesight or hearing may not be as strong will enjoy the event as well."

One client cried when Cornell explained his reasoning. "I would have never thought about my nana who can't walk if you had not asked that question," that client had said. "We would not have built an experience where she would have had fun as well. Thank you."

When planning your wedding you are in the midst of creating your own very special moment. As a result, as a bride or groom you are generally wrapped up in yourself—something that is expected, but that can lead you to soon forget about your guests. As Cornell explains it: *We are also inviting people to share in that moment. So how are we creating an environment for all guests to actually participate in that moment as well?*

Cornell's wedding planning story reminds me about the question of how we can build an inclusive culture. What matters is not that you invite people who have disability or mobility issues or who can't see or hear well. What matters is the experience you create for them. Have you created a workplace where they will thrive? Where they feel like they belong and not like they are the other? That is what inclusive leadership looks like: thinking about how everyone can enjoy the space you are creating.

Creating the Right Environment for Others

How much are you losing because you aren't creating the right environment for others to thrive authentically?

When I was a second-year law student at Santa Clara University, I participated in their on-campus interviews. Given the school's proximity to Silicon Valley, there were a large number of law firms participating and I was thrilled to take advantage of this program. Since I was top of my class, I received almost a dozen job interview offers. But as they were approaching, I realized that I'd never actually gone through a real job interview. I had held a variety of different summer jobs but I had gone directly from college to law school so this was all new to me. My parents were immigrants and from a working-class background so I also did not have the benefit of learning from them how I should conduct myself in a law firm job interview.

I never gave it a second thought that I was starting from behind simply because I was a first-generation professional. I was aware that I didn't know what I was doing in those interviews—what to say or how to act—but I thought that, as first-year law students, we were all in the same boat. It was comforting to read about a study that has confirmed that, as children of immigrants, professionals like me are launching their careers from a different starting line. In fact, it was these researchers—Martha Burwell and Bernice Maldonado—who coined the term "first-generation professional" (FGP), using it to define those people who have moved from working-class roots to white-collar careers. They researched over 290 professionals and found that structured initiatives such as work-study programs or ERGs provide critical stepping stones for FGPs, while non-FGPs were more likely to lean on family and friends for support and advice. This was certainly the case for me. I accessed and utilized all the resources available at my law school to prepare for those interviews. I had no network and did not know the ins and outs of a corporate setting.

As I started the process, I noticed that the firms would usually send one to two lawyers to campus for the interview. While I prepped for all of the obvious questions about my goals in life and what type of law I wanted to practice, I never thought that something else would be happening in these interviews. The interviewers were looking to see whether I would be a "cultural fit" with the firm. In those days, I had no idea what that meant, but I quickly found out that I didn't fit into many of the firms because there was nobody who looked like me there.

Of the twelve firms I interviewed with, only one sent a woman to interview me. All the others were white older men. Interview after interview, with each man I spoke to, my confidence in my abilities lessened and lessened. They were all very nice and very accomplished and I am sure they had the best intentions, but I could not relate to them. And they could not relate with me. We did not share the same interests or hobbies and we had very little in common. Our conversations felt very awkward and I thought *I* was the reason why we couldn't connect with each other. With every interview, I tried to change myself a little bit more to try to make myself more relatable to these men in the hopes it would make a difference. I had a lot riding on these interviews.

Ultimately, trying to pretend to be one of them did not pay off. I did not receive a single callback from any of the firms who sent male interviewers. What was more heart-breaking for me was to see that, while I was being rejected, my white male classmates with less stellar academic records than mine were getting multiple callbacks.

I felt like a failure.

I had one interview left. This last one was with a prominent Silicon Valley law firm that specialized in high-tech companies and was one of the top firms in the country. By this point, I had created a visual in my head of who was going to show up. Older white men with dark suits. To my surprise, two women in professional but more casual attire greeted me. I couldn't believe it. We immediately connected. We shared stories about ourselves and our upbringings. I told them about my internships and what I had learned. We laughed and enjoyed getting to know each other. I felt so much more like myself during this interview and was so grateful for the environment that these two women had created for me. In this more comfortable setting, I was able to demonstrate the value I could bring to the firm. I spoke with more confidence. I later learned that one woman was half Black and the other woman's husband was Black, so they each were in a position to understand the intersectionality of gender and race.

Out of the twelve interviews, this was the only firm that called me back, and I ultimately got the job. While I still had many challenges ahead, I often think back to that day. If that firm had not sent those two women to the on-campus interview that day, my life would have turned out differently. That position gave me the experience of a lifetime. IPOs. Mergers and acquisitions. Venture financings. Public company experience. It opened up a path for me to eventually become a general counsel, a board director and an investor. If those women had not shown up, I not only would have lost the opportunity to have a successful corporate career, the firm and my subsequent employers would have also lost out on the impact I made in each of their organizations along the way.

SELF-REFLECTION MOMENT

- Who could potentially benefit from you showing up authentically at work? A manager? A peer? An employee? List them out and take a look at their names. Think about how you showing up as your authentic self might give them permission to be their true selves at work.

- How much energy are you expending every day by *not* showing up authentically at work? What are you changing in order to fit in? Just notice how much effort that is and consider the possibility of letting it go. Sense how freeing that may feel.

Don't Prevent Someone from Having Their Ah-Ha Moment

Recognizing and acknowledging one's own privilege is hard and is oftentimes met with much resistance. Just the word "privilege" often makes people shut down or dive into explanations on why their life was just as hard or harder than someone else's life. In her book *Inclusion on Purpose*, author Ruchika Tulshyan quotes psychologist John Amaechi's explanation of privilege:

> Asking you to acknowledge your privilege does not minimize your personal hardship or suffering. It does not make your pain any less legitimate if you acknowledge someone else's pain, which by chance or birth, you find yourself free of. When it comes to white privilege, having it does not make your life easy, but understanding it can make you realize why some people's lives are harder than they should be.

Asking someone to examine their bias or privilege is hard. Showing up authentically when people might reject you is risky. People often wonder whether it's all worth it.

Is it worth it to push the envelope?

Is it worth it to say the thing that you know will make people uncomfortable?

Is it worth it to risk your social status by challenging existing systems or beliefs?

Cornell has seen for himself why it is worth it. One summer, while he was still working in academia, the State University of New York at Potsdam invited him to come up and do a training for the dining services staff. The class was to have more than a hundred people in attendance (mostly men) and was to last five hours.

If you don't know Potsdam, New York, it is a predominantly white community. Most families are living paycheck to paycheck. Because of the lack of diversity in this community, Cornell knew that he could not jump straight into a conversation about race because he felt they may not be in a position to receive it. So, he started the program by talking about gender and economic class. They immediately got it. They could see how biases could exist based on your economic class or gender. Then, for the second half of the program, Cornell dove into other dimensions of identity, which included race. While he knew it could backfire, he decided to show a video that talked about white privilege. When the video finished, he looked around the room and immediately noticed the faces at one table full of white women. They were visibly upset.

"You look upset. Are you okay?" he asked.

One woman spoke up. "No, I am not, Cornell. What is this thing about white privilege? What are you talking about? That is not even a real thing."

"Okay." Cornell paused, thinking of way to convey this concept. After a moment, he responded, "You understand what I mean by male privilege, right?"

"Yes, of course, I do but... Oh. I get it now."

The woman had an ah-ha moment right in front of his eyes.

"*I don't recognize white privilege because I benefit from it.* Obviously, I recognize male privilege because I know what it feels like to live in a male-dominated world. I don't recognize white privilege because I don't see it."

Cornell smiled. "Exactly."

"Oh my goodness. I never thought about it that way."

In an instant, this white woman from working-class Potsdam had a transformation. She was now open to learning more about white privilege and how it impacts our society. She was also an influencer to everyone around her at the table. It had a ripple effect. And one hundred and twenty-five new people had a next-level understanding on what racism and white privilege means. If Cornell had not pushed the envelope that day, if he had not taken the risk that the attendees would be displeased with his training, then that woman in attendance would not have had her ah-ha moment.

Don't be afraid to push the envelope. If you don't, you could be preventing someone from having their ah-ha moment.

The Benefits of Belonging at Work

For anyone who has had to downplay a part of their identity or spend energy on changing something about themselves to fit in at work, you know intuitively that there is a cost. You feel it every day when you take your deep breath and brace for the day ahead before you enter the workplace. According to Toon Taris, a professor of work and organizational psychology at Utrecht University in the Netherlands who has researched the subject, "suppressing part of one's identity can give rise to serious issues . . . it's correlated with boredom and burnout; it's also been found to increase perceptions of colleague discrimination, which can lead to lower job satisfaction and thoughts of quitting." This can have a dramatic impact on a company's business. In fact, according to a recent study by Accenture, U.S. companies alone are leaving $1.05 trillion dollars on the table by not being more inclusive.

In contrast, research has also shown that higher levels of authenticity at work relate to higher levels of employee well-being. According to a 2019 study published in the *Journal of Psychology*, "employees who perceived their selves as authentic showed higher levels of engagement. Moreover, authenticity at work and job satisfaction were positively associated. Authentic workers displayed higher levels of satisfaction at work." In contrast, the study also showed that employees who did not feel in touch with themselves or with the values and beliefs at their workplace were more emotionally exhausted, more cynical and experienced higher levels of boredom.

The data is clear. Being your authentic self at work matters. It matters because you feel better at the end of the day. You will not have wasted emotional energy on trying to be something you are not. You are investing in your own mental health.

It matters because others are watching you. If you show up authentically, you could be empowering someone else to do the same. This creates a ripple effect.

It matters because it leads to a better and more engaged workforce. When your employees are able to be themselves at work, they are connected and contributing.

It matters.

MANAGER STRATEGIES

As a leader, you have an important role to play in both building up a more diverse leadership team and in being a role model to show others that you can lead as your authentic self. Here are a few tips for doing just that.

Bring your whole self to work. Oftentimes we only bring our professional side to work. But humans are not one-dimensional, we are multi-dimensional—and in today's remote work environment, establishing connection is even more crucial. By bringing your whole self to work, you give permission to your employees to do the same. Take time off during the day to exercise, rest or meditate, and let everyone know about it. Spend the weekend hiking and generously share those pictures at work. Openly express sadness, fear or disappointment when you are facing challenging moments. The more vulnerable you are and the more you bring your whole self to work, the more others around you will do the same, and contribute to a culture of belonging.

Be intentional about diversifying your leadership team. Many companies have put in place diversity metrics, but if you peel back the onion you will often see that the numbers at the top are not changing. When you start with diverse leadership, everything flows from there. Diverse leaders are connected into a diverse network, increasing your funnel of qualified candidates. You will also be more successful at recruiting diverse talent if they can see someone like themselves on the leadership team.

Audit your interview process. Is your interview process inclusive enough? Do you have diverse interview panels? Have you reviewed your job descriptions to remove bias or unnecessary qualifications? Are you sourcing from diverse organizations to widen the candidate pool? Have you made your interview space accessible for candidates with disabilities? Be intentional about creating a process that is inclusive of different people and identities. If you have the same people with the same background interviewing candidates, you will receive the same homogenous result. Finally, ensure that all interviewers have training on how to prevent interview bias. We all have biases and we need to learn to recognize and avoid them when making hiring decisions.

Closing Note

A New Vision for You and the World

RECENTLY, I received a call from Lupe, a woman I have mentored for over a decade.

"I have two job offers," she said. "The one I want is the right stage and industry, but I am nervous that I can't be my real self there. I feel like I might always have to be proving that I belong. The other company is much more welcoming and felt like I place where I could be relaxed and more myself. However, it is not in the industry or stage that I would like and does not offer the same career opportunities that I was hoping for. Which should I choose?"

I was in the process of writing this book when the call came in. Lupe and I spent some time talking about each position, the pros and cons. We thought about the type of work she was interested in doing and where she wanted to go in her career. Neither was perfect, but one company was at a stage that was perfectly aligned with certain career goals she had at the time.

"If I felt 100-percent comfortable showing up authentically and asking for what I want and need, it would be a no-brainer," she told me.

She had one more meeting with the CEO before she had to make her decision.

"What if in this next meeting with the CEO you showed up as your authentic self and asked for what you wanted?" I asked. "What if instead of pretending to be okay with what they are offering, you were simply yourself right from the get-go and let them know what you need? No more hiding, pretending or proving?"

Lupe let out a sigh of relief. The perfect job where she could grow professionally but at the same time be her authentic self. This is exactly what she wanted, but she had legitimate fears.

Lupe is a first-generation Latina who has always hustled to try to prove that she belongs in the room. She graduated from an Ivy League school, but you would never know it because she never mentions it. It is as if she doesn't believe she earned that degree. Like me, she has faced microaggressions in the workplace throughout her career, each sending her the message that her authentic self might not be welcome. This led to a nasty bout of imposter syndrome. As a result, she was still in a state of shock that both of these companies were vying for her for their top legal spot. Of course, I was not surprised at all that she was being heavily recruited. She was a highly qualified candidate.

Lupe's story follows the journey in this book.

First, she noticed what challenges and obstacles she had overcome as a woman and a Latina in the legal profession. She learned how deep her imposter syndrome was and found ways to combat it. She took some time off work to rest before jumping into the next big role, realizing that she needed to lean into the contraction phase of the wave before launching into the expansion phase. And she took stock of what tools she had in her toolbox, noticing that one of her strongest was having a sponsor and a mentor who understood her and was advocating for her along the way. That person was me.

When I first met Lupe ten years earlier, I didn't realize what my role in her life would be or what impact she would have on mine. I also did not know that helping Latinas and anyone else who has ever felt marginalized or invisible was going to be my life's purpose. At the time, I was still hustling in my own career and she was just getting started in hers.

I remember the moment I walked into the room to interview Lupe for the first time. Her resume spilled over with top credentials and achievements. She was smart, focused and had a knowing about her that intrigued me. As we chatted, she revealed that she had recently had a baby and that her current job was not providing her with the support she needed. She was looking for a place where she could grow her career and be a mother at the same time. Wow, did I understand that feeling.

Lupe was a lot like me. She had dark brown hair, brown skin and a surname that all pointed to the fact that she was Latina, although I didn't ask. As we continued talking, I felt like I was looking at a younger version of myself. She had ambition and drive but intuitively knew that the whole motherhood-plus-career thing was going to be tough. I admired how she was so honest with me about the life she envisioned for herself. I never could have done that.

I decided to hire her and that day a special friendship and sponsorship began.

Through the years, Lupe has followed me from company to company. Well, mostly I have dragged her with me because, frankly, I couldn't do my job without her. She gave birth to her second son while she was working with me, and I was determined that she would have a different experience than I did. Instead of feelings of shame and guilt about expanding her family, she experienced joy and connection as we celebrated her pregnancy. On her request, I also extended her maternity leave from three to six months so she could spend more time bonding with her newborn son. In the grand scheme of things, that time off didn't matter to me or to the company. We all survived. You always do. But to Lupe it made all the difference. She was able to spend precious time with her baby without the pressure of having to get back to work, and she was reenergized instead of depleted when she returned. Without knowing it, she had leaned into the contraction phase during this time. When she returned to work, she continued to be the superstar she was before. She has a relentless work ethic and is always eager to learn new things. Every time I gave her a new project, she quickly became a subject-matter expert. She eventually became my right-hand person on all things.

Along the way, I knew that Lupe was destined to be a general counsel, the top role in a legal profession. But Lupe herself never thought she could do it. That nasty imposter syndrome again. She always came up with a "laundry list" of reasons why she was not cut out for the job.

I don't have the right experience. Look at these things I haven't done.

They want someone who has a broader skill set than me.

I'm not ready.

It will be too many hours and don't think I can handle it.

The list went on and on. I would just smile when she would rattle off her reasons to me. I would explain why I believed she could. I would tell her I understood how she felt, but she should still remain open to the possibility that she could do it one day. I was patient. I knew in my heart she would eventually become a general counsel and that it would just take some time for her to believe this for herself. I would give her that knowing smile when we would finish these conversations and she knew exactly what I was thinking: *You know you are going to be general counsel one day, don't you?* Then we would just laugh. She knew I wasn't going to give up on her. Sponsors don't give up.

So, did Lupe have the courage to show up authentically during that last interview with the CEO? "I just met with the CEO and shared some of my concerns and he listened," she told me. "We had a great conversation and he agreed with what I had to say. He assured me that he could make the change I had requested. Thank you so much for providing the guidance to be my authentic self. *It was nerve-wracking but also very empowering.*"

A huge smile poured over my face. I was happy not only because she got the job, but also, more importantly, because she had the courage to show up as her authentic self. It was " terrifying, but she did it. That small step right at the beginning of her relationship with the CEO could set the stage for her new career at this company.

She would no longer have to change anything about herself when she shows up at work.

She would no longer have to expend energy having to prove she belongs at the table.

She would no longer have to keep her thoughts and opinions hidden for fear of being dismissed or ignored.

This was a major turning point for Lupe. By believing in her own worth, she let others believe in her too. In that moment, Lupe realized that belonging begins with self-acceptance.

This can happen to you too.

Lupe's ability to get to self-acceptance and show up authentically during her interview not only impacts her, it impacts everyone around her.

I'm not saying this is going to be risk-free. Lupe may not stay in that organization. The unwelcoming culture there may be too ingrained. But if we don't try, if we don't repeatedly push against closed doors, we'll never shove them open.

Whatever happens for Lupe next, take a moment to think about what a monumental impact her decision could potentially have on her new company and what value it could bring to the organization.

● She will be the only Latina in the C-suite. Currently, less than 2 percent of general counsels are Latinas and she will be one of those very few. As she sits in that role, other women of color, particularly Latinas, will be able to see themselves in a position of leadership. They will be empowered to strive for similar positions in their own careers, simply because they see her in that role. Representation matters.

● She is a working mom, raising two kids in elementary school during the pandemic. She has had to juggle the impossibility of Zoom school while still holding down a job. Imagine the gains to all working parents and caregivers in that company that will come by having her around the table when employee benefits or parental leave decisions are being discussed.

● She will bring her decades of valuable corporate and operational experience to this company, propelling them to growth and success. Imagine what this company would be losing out on if she passed on it or didn't stay simply because asking for what she needed might not be well received. A workplace culture where her opinion matters was so important to Lupe that she was willing to take another job if she didn't have the sense that she could be herself. How many phenomenal employees are companies missing out on because those people feel like they may not belong?

By living her life openly and with full transparency, Lupe can give others permission to bring their full authentic selves to work. And this amazing cycle will continue.

Lupe is now stepping into the next phase of her journey. She took the small (but enormous) step of showing up authentically in this new job. Her true self earned that spot. Her willingness to be vulnerable in that moment opened the door to an amazing professional opportunity. By taking the chance to show up in a new role as herself, she is carving a pathway for all of us to step into our power and make the impact we need to see, within our organizations and within the world.

It's now your turn.

If you have followed the journey in this book, you have come to embrace and love what makes you different and how much value your unique lived experience brings to the world.

You have a new sense of awareness of why things may have been hard for you and why you have feelings of self-doubt.

You have reflected on why you may have experienced periods of physical and emotional exhaustion.

You have realized that it is also okay to choose yourself at times when the journey is too hard.

You have also learned that we go through periods of expansion and contraction in our lives and you can give yourself permission to rest when you need to.

When you emerge from this period of self-reflection and rest, a new You will arise.

The You that no longer feels inadequate or not enough.

The You that embraces the difference in you and is finally able to share that part of your identity with the world.

The You that has let go of trying to please others, and instead is focused on pleasing herself.

We need that You in the workplace.

We need the You that is unabashedly your authentic self. When we see others being their authentic selves, it gives us permission to be our own authentic self.

So, are you ready?

The world needs the real You.

Sí se puede.

Acknowledgments

WRITE A book?"

That was the subject heading of an email I received out of the blue on October 8, 2020, from Heather Kernahan and Lindsay Riddell. We were in the middle of the pandemic and I was trying to make sense of the world around me, like everybody else. *This must be a sign from the universe,* I thought to myself, so I wrote a book. Thank you to Lindsay for sending me the email, to Heather for your vision to start the "Group of 10" of first-time female authors and to all the women in our group. This book would not exist without us beginning this journey of authorship together.

When I decided to write a book, I didn't want to write just any book. I wanted to write a book that would be transformational. A book that could make an impact. I am certain that it would not have been possible without the guidance and expertise of editor and publishing strategist AJ Harper. Thank you AJ for the hours, months and now years you've spent with me in developing something I am so deeply proud of. And of course thank you to the entire family (and it is truly a family!) at the Top Three Book workshop, especially to Laura Stone for always being there to answer questions and provide emotional support when I needed it. A warm hug and thanks also to all the authors in Top Three, especially Mara Yale, Gena Cox, and Ellen Taffe, who provided me with their advice, tips, and suggestions along the way. Writing sprints make a difference!

Thank you to my publisher, Page Two, especially Trena White, who took a chance on an unknown first-time author. Publishing a book seemed so daunting to me, but the entire team at Page Two made it feel seamless. Special thanks to my editor Emily Schultz; project manager Rony Ganon; marketing whiz Meghan O'Neill; fabulous designer Jennifer Lum; and my impeccable copy editor Melissa Edwards.

A very special thanks to all the people who shared their personal stories with me, including Alexandra Navarro, Tammy Ramos, Elena Donio, Lynn Vojvodich, Jaleel McKay, Cornell Verdeja-Woodson and Zahra Langford. Thank you for trusting me with your story and for your vulnerability to share it with the world. Your stories will make a difference.

Thank you to all my male mentors and sponsors throughout my career, especially David Schellhase, Brooke Seawell, Frank Bien, Andy Chmyz and Mark Garrett, who have believed in me, shown me the ropes and helped me climb the corporate ladder. Thank you for inviting me to the table.

Thank you to Julie Castro Abrams and Erika Cramer and all the fearless women at How Women Lead. You have helped me see what impact I could have in this world and taught me how to become unabashedly visible in ways I never knew I could.

To Deborah Allen and Dr. Rachel, thank you for being my healers. You helped me during some of the darkest days of my life and without you I would not have been able to reach the other side and share my journey. Thank you for the work you do in this world to heal others.

To all my advance readers, who took the time to read this book and provide me with their valuable feedback, thank you, thank you! You made this book *so* much better!

To my dear friends Michele and Gina, thank you for being authentically you, which allowed me to do the same. Your unconditional friendship made me grow in ways I could not have imagined. I am grateful to be walking this journey called life with you every day.

Thank you to my mom and dad for sacrificing so much when they came to this country to provide a better life for me. You always put your kids first and I am forever grateful for the abundance of opportunities you afforded me. Te quiero muchismo!

And, of course, this book would not be possible without the endless support of my husband Derek and daughters Sophia and Marissa. You have encouraged and supported me throughout this whole process. Not only did you give me the space and time I needed to write, you would also lift me up when I thought I couldn't do it. To Derek, thank you for being my partner in life and the one person who I know will always be there for me. You believe in me far more than I believed in myself. I could not have done this without you. And to my two beautiful daughters Sophia and Marissa: you inspire me every day with your resilience, confidence and courage. While you may be tired of hearing my "life lessons" all the time, you actually teach me life lessons every day. This book is for you.

Notes

CHAPTER 1

76 percent of Latinos expend energy... Noni Allwood and Laura Sherbin, *Latinos at Work: Unleashing the Power of Culture* (Center for Talent Innovation, 2016).

"Because true belonging only happens... Brené Brown, *The Gifts of Imperfection: Let Go of Who You Think You're Supposed to Be and Embrace Who You Are* (Hazelden Publishing, 2010).

inclusive leaders recognize the influence... Melissa Majors, *The 7 Simple Habits of Inclusive Leaders: A Guilt-Free Guide on How to Boost Innovation and Performance by Involving Others Equally* (independently published, 2021).

CHAPTER 2

"Why... do the children of recent... Malcolm Gladwell, "Do Parents Matter?" *The New Yorker*, August 17, 1998, https://www. newyorker.com/magazine/1998/08/17/do-parents-matter.

trying to find common ground with others... Taylyn Washington-Harmon, "Code Switching: What Does It Mean and Why Do People Do It?" Health Magazine, August 13, 2020, https:// www.health.com/mind-body/health-diversity-inclusion/ code-switching.

"*Should they suppress their...* Courtney McCluney, Kathrina Robotham, Serenity Lee, Richard Smith and Myles Durkee, "The Costs of Code-Switching," *Harvard Business Review*, November 15, 2019, https://hbr.org/2019/11/the-costs-of-codeswitching.

Black and Latino people code-switch or... Amina Dunn, "Younger, College-Educated Black Americans Are Most Likely to Feel Need to 'Code-Switch,'" Pew Research Center, September 24, 2019, https://www.pewresearch.org/fact-tank/2019/09/24/younger-college-educated-black-americans-are-most-likely-to-feel-need-to-code-switch.

Black women are 80 percent more likely... Taylyn Washington-Harmon, "Code Switching."

And those who engage in this "Scan-Evaluate-Adapt"... McCluney, "Costs of Code-Switching."

while white men can certainly start their careers... Ruchika Tulshyan and Jodi-Ann Burey, "Stop Telling Women They Have Imposter Syndrome," *Harvard Business Review*, February 11, 2021, https://hbr.org/2021/02/stop-telling-women-they-have-imposter-syndrome.

Not seeing ourselves represented... Deepa Purushothaman, *The First, the Few, the Only: How Women of Color Can Redefine Power in Corporate America* (Harper Business, 2022).

This feeling can make it... Mai Vang, "Racial Imposter Syndrome," *The Current*, Summer 2021, https://thecurrentmsu.com/2021/06/22/racial-imposter-syndrome.

We all want to belong to certain... Code Switch podcast, "Racial Imposter Syndrome: Here are Your Stories," NPR, June 8, 2017, https://www.npr.org/sections/codeswitch/2018/01/17/578386796/racial-impostor-syndrome-here-are-your-stories.

She has created a memorable... Ruchika Tulshyan, *Inclusion on Purpose* (MIT Press, 2022).

CHAPTER 3

an estimated 26 percent of adults are living... Centers for Disease Control and Prevention, "Mental Health in the Workplace: Mental Health Disorders and Stress Affect Working-Age Americans," July 2018, https://www.cdc.gov/

workplacehealthpromotion/tools-resources/pdfs/WHRC-Mental-Health-and-Stress-in-the-Workplac-Issue-Brief-H.pdf.

76 percent of Latinos stated that they... Noni Allwood and Laura Sherbin, "Latinos at Work: Unleashing the Power of Culture," Coqual, 2016, https://coqual.org/reports/latinos-at-work.

psychology professor Kevin Nadal described... Hahna Yoon, "How to Respond to Microaggressions," *New York Times*, March 3, 2020, https://www.nytimes.com/2020/03/03/smarter-living/how-to-respond-to-microaggressions.html.

CHAPTER 4

According to Network of Executive Women... Sylvia Ann Hewlett, Noni Allwood and Laura Sherbin, "US Latinos Feel They Can't Be Themselves at Work," *Harvard Business Review*, October 11, 2016, https://hbr.org/2016/10/u-s-latinos-feel-they-cant-be-themselves-at-work.

Author Ethan Kross provided... Laurie Santos (host) and Ethan Kross, "How Do I Stop Negative Self-Talk?" *The Happiness Lab* podcast, July 24, 2022, https://www.pushkin.fm/podcasts/the-happiness-lab-with-dr-laurie-santos/q-how-do-i-stop-negative-self-talk.

"waves are created by energy... National Ocean Service, "Why Does the Ocean Have Waves?" National Oceanic and Atmospheric Administration, U.S. Department of Commerce, https://oceanservice.noaa.gov/facts/wavesinocean.html.

CHAPTER 5

He says that changes that seem... James Clear, *Atomic Habits: An Easy and Proven Way to Build Good Habits and Break Bad Ones* (Avery, 2018).

CHAPTER 6

in the middle of this crisis, the women were rated... Jack Zenger and Joseph Folkman, "Women Are Better Leaders During a Crisis," *Harvard Business Review*, December 30, 2020, https://hbr.org/2020/12/research-women-are-better-leaders-during-a-crisis.

Mentors vs Sponsors SLAC National Accelerator Laboratory, "The Key Role of a Sponsorship for Diverse Talent," Stanford University, https://inclusion.slac.stanford.edu/sites/default/files/The_Key_Role_of_a_Sponsorship_for_Diverse_Talent.pdf.

"promotion is the core purpose... Katharine Mobley, "Understanding the Impact Of Mentorship Versus Sponsorship," *Forbes*, Sept 17, 2019, https://www.forbes.com/sites/forbescommunicationscouncil/2019/09/17/understanding-the-impact-of-mentorship-versus-sponsorship.

On Fortune 1000 boards only... Latino Corporate Directors Association, "California Company Boards: Governor Gavin Newsom signs AB979," https://latinocorporatedirectors.org/ca_public_company_boards.php.

CHAPTER 7

She compared the workplace... Terri Givens and Rosetta Lee, "Radical Empathy: Finding a Path to Bridging Radical Divides," Common Ground Speaker Series, October 28, 2021, https://www.commongroundspeakerseries.org/terri-givens-phd-and-rosetta-lee.

this tax is the "time, money... Lori Nishiura Mackenzie and Melissa V. Abad, "Are Your Diversity Efforts Othering Underrepresented Groups?" *Harvard Business Review*, February 5, 2021, https://hbr.org/2021/02/are-your-diversity-efforts-othering-underrepresented-groups.

CHAPTER 8

Think of aspects of your identity... Sara Gaynes Levy, "Can You Really Be Yourself at Work?" *Oprah Daily*, May 15, 2019, https://www.oprahdaily.com/life/work-money/a27457513/can-you-really-be-yourself-at-work.

63 percent of managers and 57 percent of employees... Forrester Consulting "Shifting Tides: A Report on the Changing Attitudes About Mental Health Care and the Workplace," *Modern Health*, 2021, https://join.modernhealth.com/future-of-mental-health-2021-report-forrester.html

CHAPTER 9

Her last-minute goal set a new record... ESPN,
"Mavericks, Dirk Nowitzki Win at ESPYs," July
13, 2011, https://www.espn.com/espn/story/_/
id/6767665/2011-espy-awards-winners-revealed-los-angeles.

CHAPTER 10

They researched over 290 professionals... Martha Burwell and
Bernice Maldonado, "How Does Your Company Support First
Generation Professionals?" *Harvard Business Review*, January
7, 2022, https://hbr.org/2022/01/how-does-your-company-
support-first-generation-professionals.

Asking you to acknowledge your privilege... John Amaechi,
"Privilege Blinds Us to Plight of Others Who Lack It," *Financial
Times*, November 17, 2020, as quoted in *Inclusion on Purpose:
An Intersectional Approach to Creating a Culture of Belonging at
Work* by Ruchika Tulshyan (MIT Press, 2022).

"suppressing part of one's identity... Sara Gaynes Levy, "Can
You Really Be Yourself at Work?" *Oprah Daily*, May 15, 2019,
https://www.oprahdaily.com/life/work-money/a27457513/
can-you-really-be-yourself-at-work.

U.S. companies alone are leaving $1.05 trillion... Julie Sweet and
Ellyn Shook, "Getting to Equal 2020: The Hidden Value of
Culture Makers," Accenture Research, https://policycommons.
net/artifacts/1575493/getting-to-equal-2020/2265259.

"employees who perceived their selves... Ralph van den Bosch, Toon
Taris, Wilmar Schaufeli, Marla Peeters and Gaby Reijseger,
"Authenticity at Work: A Matter of Fit?" *Journal of Psychology*
153:2, 2019, doi.org/10.1080/00223980.2018.1516185.

It's Time to Embrace the Power of You!

By now, you've probably realized how important it is to embrace your authentic self and you're ready to start on your own unique journey toward self-acceptance. You've probably also realized how much others could benefit from the self-reflection exercises, next-step encouragements and manager strategies contained in this book. So, how do you get others to come along on this journey with you?

Here are four ways to get started:

Copies for your whole team: Buy copies of *Embrace the Power of You* for your team and I'll send you a free slide presentation you can use to facilitate a group discussion.

Copies for your whole organization: Contact me about bulk discounts and special offers so you can purchase this book for everyone at your organization.

Speaking at your event: Are you looking for someone to serve as a role model to your organization? Your employees? Your students? The next generation? Think of me as your first step when you are coordinating your next annual event, team offsite or retreat.

Training sessions for employees and leaders: Need a little more than inspiration to train your leaders on the importance of inclusion and authenticity? Bring Embrace the Power of You training into your organization, virtually or in person.

Let's Start the Conversation

Send me an email or reach out on social to discuss these options for your team and organization. I can't wait to hear from you!

contact@triciatimm.com
🐦 @tricia_timm
in linkedin.com/in/ptimm

About the Author

TRICIA MONTALVO TIMM is a first-generation Latina who rose through the ranks of Silicon Valley advising high-tech companies big and small, culminating in the sale of data analytics software company Looker to Google for $2.6 billion. Tricia is one of the few Latinas to have attained the triple achievement of reaching the C-suite, joining the boardroom and cracking the venture capital ceiling. Her career has spanned from working with some of the world's largest and most well-known publicly traded multinational companies to stepping on as the first lawyer at several high-growth start-ups. Tricia currently serves on the board and chairs the compensation committee at Salsify, a business-to-business SaaS company whose commerce experience management platform helps brand manufacturers, distributors and retailers collaborate to win on the digital shelf. She is also an advocate for women and girls and serves as a mentor, advisor and, more recently, investor in female-founded companies. Tricia's industry recognitions include the 2020 Women of Influence and Latino Business Leadership awards from *Silicon Valley Business Journal* and the title of Diversity Champion from the Silicon Valley Business Journal Corporate Counsel Awards.

Tricia lives with her husband and their two daughters, Sophia and Marissa, in Scotts Valley, California. Connect with her at triciatimm.com.